THE
Healing Touch

{ STORIES *from* HOPE HAVEN }

THE
Healing Touch

PAM HANSON

&

BARBARA ANDREWS

Guideposts
New York, New York

Stories from Hope Haven is a registered trademark of Guideposts.

Copyright © 2011 by Guideposts. All rights reserved.

No part of this publication may be reproduced, stored in a retrieval system or transmitted in any form or by any means, electronic, mechanical, photocopying, recording or otherwise, without the written permission of the publisher. Inquiries should be addressed to Guideposts, ATTN: Rights & Permissions Department, 16 E. 34th St., New York, NY 10016.

The characters, events and medical situations in this book are fictional, and any resemblance to actual persons or occurrences is coincidental.

Scripture are taken from *The Holy Bible, New International Version.* Copyright © 1973, 1978, 1984 International Bible Society. Used by permission of Zondervan Bible Publishers.

www.guideposts.org
(800) 932-2145
Guideposts Books & Inspirational Media

Cover design and illustration by Lookout Design, Inc.
Interior design by Lorie Pagnozzi
Typeset by Aptara

Printed and bound in the United States of America
10 9 8 7 6 5 4 3 2 1

*To the nurse in our family,
Royale Andrews.*

Stories from Hope Haven

The Best Medicine by Anne Marie Rodgers

Chasing the Wind by Patricia H. Rushford

Hope for Tomorrow by Patti Berg

Strength in Numbers by Charlotte Carter

A Simple Act of Kindness by Pam Hanson & Barbara Andrews

The Heart of the Matter by Leslie Gould

Well Wishes by Anne Marie Rodgers

Measure of Faith by Patricia H. Rushford

Cherished Memories by Patti Berg

Christmas Miracles by Charlotte Carter

The Healing Touch by Pam Hanson & Barbara Andrews

Chapter One

ELENA HURRIED INTO THE STAFF LOUNGE AT HOPE Haven Hospital on Monday morning and was surprised to see a number of nurses milling around instead of reporting for work.

"Mrs. Rodriguez, what do you think they'll do about the flu?" The question came from a young LPN who had recently been assigned to Elena's shift in the Intensive Care Unit. The query took her completely by surprise.

"Who has the flu?" Elena asked. Her first thought was that a staff member had called in sick.

"No one yet," her friend and Cardiac Care Nurse Supervisor Anabelle Scott assured her as she joined the group. Her voice was calm, and Elena could tell it was meant to reassure those around her. "There's no reason to panic."

"But what happens when we run out of vaccine and there aren't enough beds in the hospital for all the sick people?" the same LPN asked.

Elena arched her eyebrows and looked to Anabelle for an explanation.

"It seems," Anabelle answered, "that there's a serious shortage of flu vaccine in the county. All the available supplies have been allocated to the hospital, but there isn't enough for everyone who might be vulnerable. It remains to be seen whether there will be an epidemic this late in the winter, so I suggest everyone report for work as usual."

A few nurses grumbled, but Anabelle's practical explanation effectively broke up the crowd. In a few moments, she and Elena were the only ones left in the lounge.

"Is there something to worry about?" Elena slipped out of her winter jacket and patted her dark brown hair to be sure no strands had slipped out of the ponytail she wore for work.

Anabelle frowned and fiddled with the glasses she kept on a chain around her neck. She was as slender as Elena but four inches shorter, with neatly styled salt-and-pepper hair that was on its way to turning white. The fact that she hesitated to answer alarmed Elena more than the concerns of the other staff members.

"We could have a serious problem," Anabelle admitted. "Mr. Varner stopped me on the way in and asked me to reassure any staff members who might be worried."

Elena frowned, thinking of one of her mother's favorite sayings: *Where there's smoke, there's fire*. If the hospital CEO wanted to calm staff members, the flu scare must be more than a rumor.

"Today's the last day of February," Elena said. "I thought the flu season was pretty much over."

"Apparently not," Anabelle said. "We could be hit by a really serious outbreak. Unfortunately, the vaccine has been unusually scarce this year. Far too many people waited too long to get their shots and found their doctors didn't have any vaccine left. It's so scarce that the county has asked Hope Haven to be in charge of all that remains. The physicians are all on board because it's a way to make sure the most vulnerable people receive shots."

"I guess it's good that all staff members were required to get shots last fall, but it doesn't solve the problem of a potential epidemic."

Elena couldn't help but think of her own family. Her husband Cesar had been the first to get his flu shot. As a police detective, he came into contact with too many people to neglect getting one, although he was none too crazy about shots of any kind. She was sure her granddaughter was protected. It had been strongly recommended by her school that the children have the mist so they wouldn't need shots. She couldn't remember whether her son Rafael had taken her advice and had his flu shot, but she doubted it.

"Unfortunately there's nothing we can do about it now except pray that Deerford doesn't have an epidemic," Anabelle said. "The whole state of Illinois is short on vaccine, so we can't look to the government for help. No one seems to know why there's a shortage." She glanced at her watch. "Guess it's time to get to work."

Elena was surprised to see that it was nearly seven. She took pride in never being late, but this morning it would be a near thing. "See you later then," she said, hurrying to the elevator that would take her down one floor to the Intensive Care Unit.

She tried not to think about Rafael as she began her duties for the day, but she was afraid he'd neglected to get his flu shot in spite of her reminders. He was, after all, twenty-eight years old, much too old for his mother to take him in for a shot even though he lived with them. He and his adorable six-year-old daughter had come home to Deerford after Isabel's mother Sarah had deserted them shortly after Isabel's birth. Sarah had recently come back into their lives, but Rafael and Izzy still lived with Elena. Elena loved having her son and granddaughter share their home, but she had to keep reminding herself that Rafael was an adult and not her little boy anymore.

The flu was on everyone's mind this morning. It was the main topic of conversation whenever two staff members had a moment to talk. Elena reminded the new LPN that this was only a rumor right now. The young nurse was beginning to remind Elena of the little chicken who thought the sky was falling.

When her lunch break came, Elena went down to the hospital cafeteria, looking forward to a few minutes of peace and quiet with no talk of epidemics. She chose a tuna salad on a croissant and hot tea, carrying her tray to an empty table on the far side of the busy room, but before she finished even half of her sandwich, one of her favorite people came up to her.

"Mind if I join you?" James Bell, an RN from the General Medicine and Surgery Unit, asked.

Elena smiled in welcome and nodded at an empty chair. At fifty-four, James was five and a half years older than she was and had been a friendly face when she first started working at Hope Haven. Besides being an outstanding nurse, he was a man of faith who had encouraged her to return to the church after years of neglect. He was a role model for faith-based, empathetic patient care, but he also had a great sense of humor. Since he was an avid reader and a lover of words, they'd made a game of testing his vocabulary. She loved to stump him with a word he couldn't define, but it wasn't easy to do.

"Well, is everyone in your unit panicking about a possible flu epidemic?" he asked as he settled down to his helping of shepherd's pie.

So much for getting away from disaster talk, Elena thought with an ironic smile, but she knew that James wasn't given to spreading rumors. If he was concerned, she certainly respected his opinion.

"That's putting it mildly. I even had to reprimand an LPN because she couldn't keep her mind on the day's work."

"I take it you've heard about the task force." He raised one eyebrow and looked at her with deep blue eyes.

"No. What is it?"

"Apparently the administration is taking the threat very seriously. They're putting together a task force to deal with all the demands for vaccine and the possible consequences if we do have an epidemic."

"Sounds like a good idea. Let me guess—you've been tapped for it."

"Yes. There was no way I could refuse, given how serious the situation could become. Candace has agreed to serve too," he said, mentioning another friend, Candace Crenshaw, an RN in the Birthing Unit.

"Who else will be on it?"

"The county health nurse, for sure. Not surprisingly, Penny Risser is cocoordinating the whole thing."

"Oh dear."

"She is efficient," James said with a knowing grin.

"Oh yes, she is that," Elena said sympathetically, knowing that the CEO's executive assistant wasn't easy to work with. In fact, her nickname with the staff was the Dragon because she zealously guarded access to her boss Albert Varner.

"The first meeting is later today," James said.

"Is it going to take a lot of your time?" Elena knew James's plate was already full. His wife Fern had multiple sclerosis, and much of the responsibility for their home and two teenage sons fell on him. He was also active in church and a scoutmaster, and yet, he rarely said no to a worthy cause.

"How much time it will require remains to be seen," James said, "but I couldn't refuse. A flu epidemic would be really bad news. I would much rather work on preventive measures than be involved in a full-fledged epidemic."

James finished his lunch rather quickly and then excused himself to phone his wife. Elena slowly finished her own meal. She was usually refreshed by a few minutes of solitude; but today her mind was anything but tranquil. James was the last person to react to rumors or panic when things went wrong. As a veteran of the first Gulf War, he could handle almost any situation, including his wife's debilitating illness. If he was concerned, so was Elena.

Elena was standing to leave when she heard the sharp click of heels coming toward her. Medical staff members wore rubber-soled shoes or other quiet footwear, and Elena could think of only one person whose walk sounded like she was warming up for an Irish dance.

"Good morning, Penny," Elena was quick to say when the CEO's executive assistant reached her table.

"Closer to afternoon," Penny corrected her. "Can I have a minute of your time?"

Elena plopped back down on her chair, a bit surprised that she asked. Usually Penny assumed that her business took precedence over anyone else's.

"Sure, that's about how long I have before my lunch break is over." Some nurses shook in their shoes when Penny approached them, but Elena wasn't one of them. She'd been at Hope Haven for too many years.

The executive assistant didn't sit. Elena suspected that she liked towering over her. Although Penny was younger than Elena, whose hair had yet to start turning white, Penny had tight graying curls that did nothing to flatter her rather sallow complexion. The woman had one passion—growing plants and flowers—but her love of floral beauty hadn't carried over into her style choices. Today she was wearing a gunmetal-gray suit that made her look like a character in a sci-fi movie. Her mood wasn't any cheerier.

"You've probably heard about the flu scare," Penny said.

"I've heard a lot of rumors, yes, but I'm not sure what to believe."

"Believe." Penny cleared her throat as though preparing to make an important announcement. "There's not enough vaccine anywhere in the county, and Deerford may be vulnerable to an epidemic. Mr. Varner has given me the job of putting together a task force." Using her boss's name, she made it sound like a presidential appointment.

"So I've heard," Elena said.

"I'd like you to serve on the task force. Mr. Varner recommended you."

"I'm not sure what I have to contribute."

Penny waved away Elena's hesitation. "We're meeting in the conference room as soon as your shift is over. Please be there. I trust I can tell Mr. Varner that you're on board."

At least she said please, Elena thought. "I'll be there." Mentally, she rearranged her family situation as Penny nodded and walked away. She took her calling as a nurse and a Christian too seriously to refuse being of service in a potential crisis.

Rafael would have to get off work early to pick up Izzy from school, usually something Elena did on her way home from work. She was sure it would be all right, though, because he was working at Baldomero, her mother's Mexican restaurant in downtown Deerford. Certainly Camila Baldomero wouldn't object to letting her grandson leave early to pick up his daughter.

Izzy loved to sit on a stool in the restaurant kitchen and watch her great-grandmother cook, often sampling little tidbits. That would pretty much take care of her appetite for dinner, and Cesar could heat up the casserole left from yesterday if she was too late to fix anything else. Her husband sometimes grumbled at leftovers, but his detective work often kept him too busy for lunch, and he'd eat anything when he was hungry enough.

Heading back to work, she continued to mull over the flu scare. If there was a serious epidemic, the hospital's resources would be taxed sorely. There had been deaths in other states from the current strain of flu, and she could hardly imagine how the hospital would isolate an onslaught of flu cases and still provide services for other patients. The more she thought about it, the more important the task force seemed. She was a great believer in preparedness, and Hope Haven Hospital certainly wasn't ready for a major outbreak. Cesar's eating warmed-over casserole was a small price to pay if there was anything she could do to help get ready for a potential disaster.

Candace Crenshaw looked in on the newly delivered mother, rewarded by a wan smile. Caroline Baker had just had her first child at age forty-one, and it had been a long hard labor. Much as she admired the patient's courage and determination to begin motherhood in her forties, Candace felt extremely grateful that she and her late husband Dean had had children when they were young. Dean had died unexpectedly nearly five years ago at the age of thirty-six, and she didn't know what she would have done without their two children to give her purpose amidst the sorrow she had felt.

Thinking of her son Howie, recently turned seven, and her daughter Brooke, who was looking forward to her thirteenth birthday in a few weeks, reminded Candace that she needed to call her mother once her shift ended. Janet had moved in with them after Dean's death, and Candace was exceedingly grateful for her help. Divorced when Candace was in middle school, her mother was a retired school media specialist and a wonderful grandmother. She would be there when the children got home from school, of course, but Candace needed to warn her to go ahead with dinner if the task force meeting lasted too long.

She didn't have a clue what to expect, except that Penny had made the flu situation sound urgent. Much as she liked to spend time with the kids after work, she couldn't refuse the opportunity to help make plans for a possible epidemic. Her patients, both mothers and newborns, would be especially vulnerable.

Penny hadn't said why she'd been selected, but she could only assume that she would be there to represent the Birthing Unit. Her supervisor Riley Hohmann seemed a more logical choice, but perhaps she'd declined to serve. Or, more likely, she was already so bogged down with responsibilities that she didn't have time to take on what could be a very time-consuming job.

Candace checked out at three and hurried to the staff lounge to make a quick call to her mother on the cell phone in her purse. She felt immensely grateful that her children had had flu mist and were protected, but she worried because her mother had decided against a shot. Janet had had Asian flu when they first started naming the virus in the late 1950s. A fifth grader then, Janet remembered that half of her school had been out sick at the height of the epidemic, both students and teachers. She was relying on the immunity she got from that severe outbreak to protect her, but Candace still worried about her.

Candace offered up a prayer that their precautions wouldn't be necessary and then hurried to make her call so she wouldn't be late for the first meeting of the task force. Would it be an exercise in preparedness or the crucial first step in getting ready for a real crisis?

Chapter Two

ELENA WAS ONE OF THE LAST TO ARRIVE IN THE conference room where the task force was meeting. Because all her patients were critical, she couldn't always rush away on the dot of three when her shift officially ended. Today a surgery patient had gone septic, and she'd had to supervise her removal to isolation. The meeting was already under way when she quietly entered the room and found a vacant chair at the long table. Penny frowned at her tardiness but didn't stop talking.

She found herself sitting between Candace and the county health nurse Maxine Newman, a sweet-faced woman in her midfifties. Elena knew her casually, and she'd occasionally had conferences with her husband, the high school vice principal, when Rafael had managed to get himself in trouble as a student. The couple's only son was in pharmacy school in Michigan, and she remembered a conversation she'd once had with Maxine about the difficulties of raising an only child.

Maxine gave her an understanding smile. She'd worked at Hope Haven as a young RN and knew there were situations beyond the control of a nurse.

Penny was winding down her long preamble. When she introduced the county health nurse, Elena realized that Maxine would be the real head of the task force. No one in the room, not even Dr. Hamilton with his long years of medical experience, was more qualified to coordinate disaster preparations.

Maxine was medium height, neither heavy nor thin, and had a halo of light brown hair around her pleasantly round face. Even in a flared navy skirt and white uniform blouse with a logo over the pocket, she didn't look like an authority figure, but Elena knew looks could be deceiving. The county health nurse had a well-deserved reputation for getting things done. Maybe no one else noticed, but Penny stepped aside a bit reluctantly. Elena was relieved to know a public health–expert would be guiding them.

"As I see it, Hope Haven has a threefold responsibility," Maxine said, speaking in a gentle but persuasive voice. "First, you need to distribute the limited supply of vaccine to those who are most vulnerable. You need to establish guidelines to decide who gets shots. Dr. Hamilton, would you be so kind as to head up a subcommittee to determine the criteria?"

"Happy to," the distinguished silver-haired physician said.

"Thank you. Second, there needs to be a plan to handle a large number of critical cases, should it be necessary. Flu patients will have to be isolated from the general population; and no visitors can be allowed in the hospital, even if it means drawing extra security from local law enforcement."

"Do you think things will get that serious?" Penny asked.

"No, but we have to be prepared for the worst possible situation. I've already spoken to James Bell, and he's agreed to head a group that will formulate emergency plans," Maxine said, looking toward James who gave an affirmative nod.

There were approving looks on both sides of the table, a measure of how much James was respected.

"The third major responsibility is keeping the public informed. We need to hammer home how important simple hygiene is and, at the same time, stress the seriousness of an epidemic without causing panic."

"What about the schools?" a woman from radiology asked. "Will they be closed?"

"I'll be in constant contact with the superintendent about closing the schools if necessary. As I was about to say, my office will handle public information, but I am asking a few of you to help. Right now, the number one priority is to spread factual information and combat rumors." Elena knew she was right about that. A few staff members were already panicky, and it would get worse before this was over.

"Mr. Varner and I have had a long discussion about personnel and have come up with suggestions on how each of you can best help. With Penny's input, of course," she added diplomatically.

Copies of the assignments were passed around, and Elena was happy to be working on public information with Maxine. Anabelle would be working with Dr. Hamilton, and Candace was on James's committee.

Elena left the task force meeting without a clear idea of what she could contribute, but no doubt she'd be hearing from Maxine soon.

As she approached her house, Elena was excited to tell Cesar about the task force. Maybe he would have some idea of why she'd been appointed to the information committee. She smiled, anticipating what he'd have to say. It was a running joke between them that she could talk nonstop for hours on end when she was fired up about a cause, and it was another joke altogether that she never said no to joining a cause.

Cesar's red truck wasn't in their driveway, which wasn't terribly surprising. As a police detective, he occasionally worked overtime, or he might have gone to the library to study for the course he was taking online. Rafael's battered white van, used to haul his band's instruments on their weekend gigs, was parked there, and Elena tried to think of the best way to suggest that he get a flu shot at the hospital as soon as possible.

She shivered in the cold wind that was picking up, carrying a dusting of snow in its wake. Much as she anticipated the arrival of spring, it looked like they were due for more wintry weather. Sometimes she longed for the blazing sun of summer.

"Hello," she called out as she came into her cozy kitchen. "Anybody home?"

"Just me," Rafael said, coming into the room. "Dad left a note. He and Izzy were too hungry to wait for you, so they went out for pizza."

"I guess that leaves the leftover casserole for you and me," she said, shrugging out of her heavy jacket.

"Sorry, Mom."

He gestured at the empty dish soaking in the sink, a sheepish smile on his handsome face. He had his father's dark, sometimes mischievous eyes; and she loved the way they sparkled when he was happy.

Her son was happy, she realized. He'd been depressed and unhappy for such a long time that seeing his contentment was like sunshine to Elena. He delighted in his daughter and was focused on becoming a police officer like his father after years of uncertainty about his future. "How did your class go today?" she asked, rubbing her hands together to warm them.

"Great. It's nearly the end of the semester, so I'm eager to see what grade I'll get. If it's good, it will look good on my résumé when I start applying for police jobs."

After much soul-searching, Rafael had decided that he wanted to follow in his father's footsteps and become a police officer. When he finished his community college courses, he was going to start applying for jobs. It could be a long process; and when he was hired, he would be sent to a police academy for training. Both of his parents gratefully supported his decision, glad that his uncertainty about his future was resolved.

"There's no reason why you can't get an A," the proud mother in her said. "You have a good head."

"When I use it, you mean," he said with a broad grin.

"Speaking of using your head," Elena said, taking the opportunity that had arisen, "you really should have a flu shot. There's a possibility we might have a flu epidemic in the county. That's why I'm late coming home today. I'm on a task force to help prepare for it."

"It's almost spring, Mom. I'll be fine."

"Rafael," she said in a stern voice. "You can still listen to your mother. Flu shots are in short supply; but if you become eligible for one, I want you to promise to get one."

"But, Mom, with you on the job, the flu wouldn't dare invade Deerford," her son teased.

"I'm serious," Elena protested. "Promise me you'll have the shot if I can get one for you."

Usually she worked hard to treat her son as an adult. He'd been left with a baby to care for by himself, and it had been a blow to his pride to move back with his parents, however supportive they were. On this issue, though, Mother still knew best.

"You win," Rafael said with a smile. "I'll brave a cold steel dagger if it will put your mind at ease."

"A tiny pinprick," she admonished him, returning his smile and grateful that he'd agreed.

Rafael headed to his room to study, and Elena decided to open a can of soup for supper. But before she could open the can, the kitchen door flew open, announcing her husband and granddaughter's return.

In her long marriage that had begun when she was only nineteen, one thing hadn't changed. She still felt a rush of happiness when her handsome husband came home. She often fretted over the dangers of his job as a detective, and it was always good to have him back in the security of their house.

He pulled her into his arms and gave her a warm kiss before slipping out of his winter jacket.

Izzy stood still for a quick hug and then ran off to tell her father about pizza with her grandfather. Elena watched her beautiful, dark-haired little granddaughter for a moment and then turned to her husband.

"So how was your day?" he asked, his black eyes sparkling in the way that told her he'd missed her.

"You're looking at a member of a task force," she said with quiet pride. "The hospital is preparing for a possible flu epidemic."

"Congratulations. They couldn't have picked a more competent nurse."

She flushed ever so slightly at her husband's compliment. "Oddly enough, I'm on the information committee."

He laughed out loud.

"What's so funny?" she said with a smile.

"Sweetheart, I can't imagine a better person to spread news."

"Are you saying I'm a gossip?" she asked with mock severity, hands on her hips.

"Not at all, only that you know how to stay on top of a situation. What I want to know is how much time this is going to take. You know that sometimes I feel like I have to make an appointment to see my own wife."

"You're exaggerating. I'm almost always here when you get home from work, not that you're always on time."

"Sometimes I have to work overtime. It's part of the job."

"I should know that after all these years. The task force is part of my job, if you want to put it that way."

"Yeah, but you find plenty of other things to take up your time. Your Wednesday night thing, for example."

"That's my Bible study night, as you well know. I'll thank you not to call it a 'thing.'"

"Sorry. I just miss you when you're gone so much, but don't worry about it. There's a basketball game I want to watch on TV tonight. Any chance you'll make some popcorn and watch it with me?"

"I'll pop the corn and maybe watch a little of the game, but I have clean laundry to fold and dirty clothes to wash. And Izzy hasn't had a home-baked cookie in her school lunch in ages. Then I have some calls to make for a potluck at church...."

"Wake me up before you go to bed if I fall asleep in my chair," he said in a disgruntled voice.

Elena sighed, feeling a little tinge of guilt. She knew that deep down he understood how hard it was to balance a full-time job and a family, but occasionally he'd acted resentful about the time she devoted to extra activities, especially anything to do with church. She prayed that someday he would come to accept the Lord as part of his life and join the community of believers. She loved him and didn't want him to be unhappy, but the church was part of her life too.

Izzy raced into the kitchen, eager to tell all about her day at school. Elena's heart swelled with love and joy, and she tried to forget Cesar's cross mood. Someday he would understand that the church could be a uniting force in their marriage. She had to believe that.

Chapter Three

James came home to find a crisis on his doorstep. His two teenage sons, Nelson and Gideon, had been out searching since dinner, but now it was getting dark. They came home looking tired and dejected.

"Dad, we looked everywhere for Sapphire," Gideon, the elder son, said.

"Yeah, we asked everyone we saw too," Nelson added. "I don't get it. How could she just disappear?"

"Maybe she got confused by our new neighborhood," James suggested.

"That's possible," Gideon said. "She's never disappeared like this before."

Sapphire was Fern's beloved Maine coon cat. She had silvery gray hair marked by darker striations. At fifteen pounds, she was an adult with several distinguishing characteristics. She had a ruff around her neck like a lion, a bushy tail not unlike a raccoon's, and six toes on her feet. More importantly, she'd never run away before. Quite the opposite, she usually came when her name was called.

"Maybe she'll show up tomorrow," Nelson said. "She has to be hungry."

"Thanks for all your effort," James said. "But don't you guys have homework?"

Nelson quickly agreed that he did have an English assignment, but Gideon sighed at the prospect.

Their father shooed them off and then walked into the family room to give his wife the bad news. Sapphire was Fern's cat, an adored companion when MS kept her home for days at a time.

She was stretched out on the couch with an unread book on her lap. Although she was nine years younger than her husband, her disease had taken a toll. There were silver strands among the brown in her pixie cut, and chronic fatigue had left her looking frail and older than her forty-four years. But to James, she was still as beautiful as ever; and he rejoiced whenever her MS showed signs of remission. Lately she'd been walking well with a cane, only using her portable wheelchair for excursions outside their home.

James took a deep breath. He knew how distressed Fern would be and hated to be the bearer of bad news.

"The boys didn't find her, did they?" she asked, guessing what he was about to tell her.

"No, they had to give up because it's too dark to see. Maybe tomorrow..."

"Maybe," she repeated without sounding hopeful.

"She isn't familiar with our new neighborhood. I called a couple of friends on our old street. They promised to be on the lookout for her in case she made her way back there."

"I know you're doing all you can, but I'm not optimistic. It's not like Sapphire to wander off. You can set your watch by her dinnertime. You know how she sits and stares at the cupboard when it's time to eat. I hope she isn't starving."

James was pretty sure Sapphire could look out for herself in that respect. If she couldn't beg a bowl of milk from some kindly soul, she still had her ancestors' hunting skills. But he didn't want to point that out to Fern. He was much more worried that their pet had lost a territorial battle with an automobile.

He got up early the next morning, hoping to find the family feline meowing outside the back door. She'd only been gone one night, so there was still hope.

Moving quietly through the kitchen and out the back door, he stood for a few moments enjoying the spacious backyard and the patio with a whirlpool tub. They'd moved from their old home to make life easier for Fern.

There was no sign of Sapphire, nor had he really expected to find her. He was also concerned that their old house hadn't sold yet, putting him in a gloomy mood as he started his day.

Elena saw James pulling into the staff parking lot as she got out of her own car Tuesday morning. On the way to work, her mind had been full of questions about the task force. This was the first day of March. Would there really be an epidemic when winter was almost over? Of course, the snow crunching underfoot made spring seem far off. She wanted to hear what James had to say about it, especially since he'd been given such a responsible job.

There was a cold wind this early in the morning, and the piles of dirty snow that ringed the parking lot showed no sign of melting away any time soon. Maybe if they could get through this month, the flu threat would pass them by. She prayed that the severe strain wouldn't claim any victims, here or anywhere else.

"Good morning," James said as he left his car and walked toward her.

"Hi. Glad I caught you before our shift starts. What do you think of the task force? Do you really think we'll need emergency measures?" she asked.

"It's good to be prepared, even if there isn't a crisis situation. In fact, we should be familiar with disaster procedures even if we never need to use them."

"I agree," Elena said. "I just wondered whether you've seen reports from other parts of the country. How real is the threat?"

"Very real," he said in a glum voice.

He didn't sound like his usual upbeat self, and she wondered whether his new responsibility was preying on his mind.

"If you're worried, then I'm in panic mode," she said, exaggerating in an attempt to cheer him up.

"Don't get hysterical," he finally teased. "I'm concerned about the possibility of an epidemic, but I'm down because my day got off to a bad start."

"Oh, I hope Fern hasn't taken a turn for the worse."

"No, thank the Lord, but I am worried about her. Sapphire is missing, and you know how Fern loves her. I was hoping the cat would show up this morning, but no luck."

"She's pretty much a house cat, isn't she?"

"Yes, but we've always been able to let her out for a little exercise. She rarely left our old yard, and she was good about coming inside when she got tired. Of course, in our other house, she had a little swinging cat door so Fern didn't have to let her in. I've been meaning to install one in our new home, but there are always so many things to keep me busy."

"I don't know how you manage to do everything you do as it is."

"My days are full," he admitted, "but the Lord has given me the strength and energy to do all that's required of me. Fortunately, I like being busy."

"Well, good luck heading the committee. I hope everyone on the staff cooperates."

"I'm sure they will when they understand how serious an epidemic could be. I guess that's your responsibility, convincing people that it could happen here."

"The county nurse has ideas on how to do that. In fact, I got a phone message asking me to meet with her after my shift. Maxine is so efficient, my job should be easy."

"No doubt she'll find jobs for you," James said with a soft chuckle, sounding more like his usual self.

Elena's morning flew by, giving her no time to wonder about her role on the task force. They had some empty beds in the Intensive Care Unit, but the patients they did have more than made up for any decrease in numbers. Among the more critical they had a man in his early sixties whose chance of survival was slim and an elderly woman who was barely hanging onto life. The families of both were in the nearby lounge hoping to spend a few precious moments with their loved ones. Visiting was strictly controlled in ICU, but when a patient was terminal, the rules were relaxed.

Comforting families wasn't an official part of Elena's duties, but she often spent a considerable amount of time keeping them informed and calm. She imagined how she would feel if someone she loved was critically ill and somehow found the right words to say to anxious relatives. Sometimes it was the hardest part of her job. She didn't know how she would do it without faith in the Lord and the promise that His suffering people would go on to a better place.

Shortly after noon, Larry, a young male nurse from the Emergency Room, wheeled a new patient into the unit on a gurney.

"Hey, I've got a Jane Doe in a coma for you," he said, stopping at the nurses' station where Elena was typing an update into the computer.

She hurried to the gurney while Larry briefed her.

"According to the ambulance driver, it was a freak accident. She was walking along a road just outside of town, facing on-coming traffic. A guy in the car coming toward her turned around to pay attention to his dog in the backseat of his car and swerved off the road. She had time to jump out of his way, but she fell down a steep slope and hit her head on a rock or something."

Elena could see the dark bruising on her arm and one side of her face, but they weren't the kind of injuries that brought a person to ICU. A head injury was.

Larry followed her into an unoccupied room and helped her move the patient onto the bed.

"The police must have some idea who she is," Elena said. "Have you seen their report?"

"I haven't, but the ambulance driver said they didn't have a clue."

"She looks to be in her late forties, maybe early fifties," she said. "How about her clothing? Was she well dressed?"

"Here's her stuff," the young man said, handing Elena a plastic bag of clothing. "All they found on her person was a key, probably a house key."

She took it and looked through it before stowing it in the cabinet in a corner of the room.

"Nothing in her pockets or her shoes," Elena said confirming what he said.

"No, she probably went out for a morning walk. Healthy thing to do, you know. Why carry a purse when you're only going to be gone for a little while? I carry only my key when I run too."

He was tall and slender with close-cropped brown hair. Elena guessed that he put in quite a few miles on a regular basis.

"She must live near the accident site. I hope someone will report her missing fairly soon." Elena could only imagine how worried her family would be if a woman her age suddenly disappeared.

"Most likely," the male nurse said as he started to leave. "Her shoes are a top brand, her clothes fairly high-end as far as I can tell. We're not dealing with a nomad. Someone will miss her."

"Good. The sooner, the better," Elena said.

Coma patients never complained and never demanded special attention. Their very existence depended on nursing skills, but they were incapable of thwarting their treatment by refusing medication or second-guessing the medical staff. Some nurses might say those in a coma were ideal patients, but they worried Elena more than any others. She was always deeply saddened by a patient in a coma. There was no way of predicting how long the condition would last. Some never woke up. Others came out of it relatively soon; but either way, there could be brain damage.

It was especially hard to deal with the family and friends of a person in a coma. They walked a fine line between fear, hope, and despair. A nurse couldn't give encouragement that might not be warranted, but it was hardwired in Elena's nature to offer comfort.

By the end of her shift, no one had come to be with the new patient. Elena noticed that she didn't wear a wedding ring, but surely someone would miss her soon. No matter how unsettling it was to tell people the truth about a comatose patient, it was worse when no one came to the hospital.

She had to put the new patient out of her mind for now. Certainly by the time she came in tomorrow, the Jane Doe would have her own name back. Someone would come forward to identify her and pray for her recovery.

Although she felt unusually tired, Elena tried to rally enthusiasm for the meeting with Maxine. Her group was meeting in the community health office, which had a rather sparsely furnished conference room with a casual arrangement of chairs around a circular table.

Penny was there ahead of her, looking even more severe than usual in a black suit with a gray turtleneck sweater. Elena had known that she would be involved and was resigned to her heavy-handed participation.

Fortunately, Quintessa Smith was also on the committee. She was the executive assistant to Hope Haven's chief financial officer, and Elena had worked with her on various projects in the past. She was only twenty-eight, but she was vivacious and ambitious. More importantly, she was an idea person, the perfect addition to the small group headed by Maxine. Today Quintessa was wearing a peach wool dress that complemented her warm cocoa complexion and expressive brown eyes. She was sitting at the table with a green folder in front of her, probably stuffed full of great ideas.

Elena realized that she was coming to the table without any of her own bright ideas. She'd been too distracted by Cesar's recent change of mood and by her unidentified coma patient to give a lot of thought to a possible epidemic.

"Thank you for coming," Maxine said to begin their meeting. She was dressed in her familiar navy skirt and white uniform top, but today she'd added a navy sweater and a pair of pearl earrings. It was impossible to look at her and not think what a pleasant person she was. Elena didn't want to let her down, so she gave her complete attention to the business at hand. She knew that without good communication, their efforts wouldn't be successful. She'd already seen how easily false rumors could circulate. "Let's start by hearing your ideas on how to keep people informed and calm," the county health nurse said.

"I don't think we should tell anyone more than they absolutely need to know," Penny said. "After all, it's the administration's responsibility. We're not here to do their job."

"We're here to make sure Hope Haven is ready for a flu emergency," Quintessa reminded her. "If we have to step on anyone's toes, it's the price we pay for preparedness."

Elena agreed with her, but hashing it over wouldn't accomplish anything. She quickly added a suggestion of her own, although she knew it wasn't anything original. "We can use the staff newsletter to keep our people informed."

"I thought we could put up some posters listing emergency procedures in places where staff members will see them like the lounge and the kitchen," Maxine said.

"We'll start a panic if patients and visitors see them," Penny said.

"That will be James's responsibility," Quintessa said, "but we also need drills to be sure everyone understands their role in any crisis, not just a flu epidemic. Maybe we can coordinate with his committee."

"We haven't been given a mandate to run the whole hospital," Penny said in a sour voice.

"We have some good suggestions," Maxine said. "Is there anything you'd like to add, Penny?"

"We need to define what constitutes an epidemic," the CEO's executive assistant said. "Is it one patient, two patients, ten patients infected with the virus?"

"That's a good point," Maxine said, "and one my office will be working on."

Elena admired her tact and patience. Maxine listened to their ideas and didn't let Penny's negative attitude interfere with their goals. She made all of them, even Penny, feel good about their suggestions, a sure sign of a good leader.

By the time the meeting broke up, everyone had assignments. Elena would be in charge of staff communications; Penny would work with the administration and hospital board; and Quintessa would handle media including newspapers, radio, and TV. Maxine would keep in contact with state and national officials, feed information to her committee, and work with them as needed.

Elena felt better than when she'd gone into the meeting. For a short time she'd forgotten family and work problems, but she felt a great need to pray for the committee's success and the welfare of her own family and patients. As she sometimes did, she stopped in the hospital chapel for a few minutes on her way out. A gray-haired man sat slumped on a front seat, perhaps praying for a loved one who was a patient. Elena was very quiet so she wouldn't disturb him, and her own silent prayers were heartfelt and sincere. Before she finished, she also asked the Lord to spare them from a flu epidemic. However prepared Hope Haven was, people would still suffer if a dangerous virus was set loose in Deerford.

Help me, dear Lord, to serve those I love and to love those I serve, she prayed silently. *Amen.*

Chapter Four

JAMES WAS SO PROUD OF HIS BOYS. WHILE HE was preoccupied with plans for the hospital's emergency procedures, they'd taken charge of the hunt for Sapphire. After their futile search Monday evening, Gideon had run off a pile of fliers on their home computer, and Nelson had enlisted his Scout troop to distribute them to stores, nail them on poles, and generally alert the whole town, not just their neighborhood.

Wednesday morning James decided to take a couple fliers to work with him. He smiled as he read what Gideon had written.

MISSING CAT

Maine Coon, long silver hair with smoky markings, a ruff like a lion and a tail like a coon. Friendly with people and answers to the name SAPPHIRE. $25 reward for her return.

Gideon had also mentioned where the cat was last seen and gave their phone number and e-mail address in case anyone spotted her. Gideon had located a photograph of Sapphire that Nelson had taken for a Scout project. It was a bit blurry, but it gave an idea of how she looked. As far as James could tell, his sons had done all that could be done, even pooling their own money to offer the reward. If their efforts didn't turn up any leads, he didn't know what else to try.

When he got to work, he pinned one of the fliers on the message board in the staff lounge. Anabelle was the first person to come over and read it.

"How sad!" she said. "Fern must be terribly worried."

"Yes, she really misses her. Neither of us is very optimistic about getting her back," James admitted. "Gideon and Nelson have taken charge of the search. I hate to see them disappointed, but Sapphire has never gone missing before this. I'm afraid she might have been hit by a car."

"Oh dear, let's hope not," she said sympathetically.

James knew that Anabelle was an animal lover, although she preferred dogs. She and Cameron had invested a lot of time and love in their "pound puppy," a rambunctious mixed breed they'd adopted, even taking him to obedience school when he proved to be a handful.

"I guess if this doesn't work," he said gesturing at the flier, "we'll never know what happened to her. I haven't suggested getting another cat yet, but it might come to that. Fern is home so much that it's good for her to have a companion like Sapphire."

"Yes, we feel the same way about Sarge. Cameron didn't especially want a dog, but now that he's retired and home quite a bit, he loves having a canine companion."

"How is Cam? Is he enjoying retirement?"

"The winter was a bit rough for him, to be honest. He has seemed a bit sluggish lately. In fact, he has a doctor's appointment today. I wish I could go with him, but he wouldn't hear of me taking a day off."

"I hope Cam gets good news from the doctor." James caught a wall clock out of the corner of his eye and realized he needed to get to work. "Well, gotta go," he said. "Let me know how things go with Cam's doctor."

"I will. Oh, I just remembered something, but I have to run as well. Are you eating in the cafeteria today?"

"Yes, I plan to."

"I'll see you there. I may have an idea to help find Sapphire." She hurried off, leaving James puzzled. He thought they'd tried everything, but he was open to suggestions, especially from Anabelle. She was one of the most resourceful people he knew.

Elena had a bad feeling when she reported for work. The first thing she did was ask Gloria Main, one of two RNs who worked the night shift in ICU, about the coma patient. If Elena were sick herself, the night nurse was the one she'd want on her case. In her late fifties, she was a sturdy, no-nonsense woman with salt-and-pepper hair and a stoic look that belied her fervent dedication to her patients. When Gloria frowned, Elena knew the news wasn't good.

"No change." Gloria's face crinkled in concern.

"She's still in a coma." Elena was only confirming the bad news. "What about her identity?"

"We don't have a clue."

"No one has reported a missing person matching her description?'

"Afraid not."

"Someone must be worried enough to call the police. People don't just disappear in Deerford."

Gloria shook her head. "Poor thing, lost in who knows what murky place in her mind, and no loved one to hold her hand or talk to her. But it's early on. She could still wake up and tell us who she is. You're right. People don't vanish into thin air. Someone will notice she's gone, maybe a neighbor or someone where she works if she lives alone."

Gloria segued into conversation about another patient, one who'd had a restless night. Elena forced herself to listen carefully to what she was saying. She was a professional, and she couldn't focus all her attention on one patient.

The morning went fast. It always did when they were busy, and most of the rooms in the ICU were in use. Elena was nearly ready to take her lunch break when she heard soft weeping coming from one of the rooms. It surprised her because Maria Acuna, a cancer survivor who'd undergone surgery, was doing very well and would soon be moved out of the unit.

"Mrs. Acuna, is something wrong?" Elena asked in her most soothing voice.

"Oh dear, I'm just being a silly old woman. I'm so grateful to the doctors for giving me a chance to live longer. I just feel bad about disappointing my granddaughter."

"I'm sure she understands and only wants you to get well."

"Yes, but I have to break my promise to her." Her round face scrunched up in misery, deepening the laugh lines by her eyes.

"What promise is that?" Elena asked sympathetically.

"She is having a quinceañera in Texas, where she lives. Do you know what that is?"

"It's a big event in a young fifteen-year-old girl's life to celebrate her coming of age," Elena said. "My family's from Texas, and I had my own quinceañera. It was a big step in growing up."

"Yes, and the girls always wear beautiful gowns, almost like wedding gowns. My son and his wife don't earn a lot of money, so I promised to make Rosa's gown. Now I won't be able to finish it in time. I have all the pieces cut out, but the doctor says I won't be strong enough to work at my sewing machine." She wiped at the dampness on her cheeks with a tissue. "She's my only granddaughter, and I'm going to fail her."

"Tell me about the dress," Elena said.

"The top is ivory lace lined with silk. My husband took me to Peoria to find just the right material. The skirt is satin and very full with little rosebuds—because her name is Rosa. I asked my cousin to finish it, but she isn't very good at sewing. She was afraid she might ruin it. But what good are a pile of pieces?"

"I have a thought," Elena said, a little apprehensive about volunteering to finish the dress. But how could she let a young girl miss her quinceañera because she didn't have a dress? "Have your husband bring all the material when he comes to visit you tonight. I'll look at what you have and see if I can finish it for you."

"You know how to work with silk and satin?" There was wonder in her voice, not doubt.

"I can't be sure until I see the pattern, but if it's not too difficult, I'll try to finish it for your granddaughter. I'm an avid sewer."

"You don't know how much it would mean to me and my Rosa. I can't thank you enough."

"I have to see it first," Elena cautioned. "How soon will she need it?"

"My brother is leaving for Texas in about two weeks. The plan was for him to take the dress with him."

"I'm not promising," she said, mentally going over her schedule, trying to find enough free time for a complicated sewing project.

"When you see how beautiful the material is, your fingers will itch to work with it," Mrs. Acuna said, smiling weakly as she blotted her watery eyes.

Elena believed that God had given her certain talents so she could do her small part to look after His people. Sewing, though, had always been her hobby, something that brought her pleasure, especially when she made pretty things for her granddaughter. Could this be part of her mission, to bring happiness to her patient by finishing a very important dress? Was she up to the task?

More importantly, what would Cesar say if she took on another time-consuming project?

When Anabelle came into the cafeteria, James was already sitting with Candace at a table. The room buzzed with lunch-hour chatter, a testimony to the good, reasonably priced meals served there. She was glad her friends' break coincided with hers. It always made her happy to spend time with them. She went through the food line and picked out a salad and a corn muffin and then went to join them.

"Ah, you're just the person we need," James said in a welcoming voice. "Candace is on the cusp of being the parent of a teenage girl. Any good advice for her?"

Anabelle laughed, although in truth, she was glad her son and two daughters were beyond the moody, unpredictable teen years. They were all good kids, but she and Cam had their ups and downs with them. She couldn't imagine how difficult life might be for a parent with rebellious, unruly children.

"That's why God gives us babies," she said. "So we can learn to love them before they hit their teens."

James laughed, but Candace only gave her a weak smile.

Anabelle could only guess how hard it must be for her as a single parent. She thanked the Lord that Cameron was such a loving husband and father. They shared a strong bond, although once in a while it was strained a little. Today she really had wanted to go to the doctor with him. She didn't think his refusal had anything to do with her taking a day off. Sometimes her husband reminded her of an ostrich with its head buried in the sand. He thought that if no one knew something was wrong, it wasn't a problem.

She sighed and settled down to her lunch, remembering what she wanted to tell James.

"If you don't have any luck finding Sapphire on your own, there is one alternative," Anabelle said.

"I'll be grateful for any suggestion," James said, putting down his fork with a bite of macaroni and cheese still on it.

"A friend of mine lost her parrot once. She'd taught it quite a few words and had gotten quite fond of it. She was really upset when it somehow got out of its cage on the back patio and disappeared. It happened in the fall, and she was afraid it couldn't survive alone, especially not when the weather started getting cold. She contacted a service called Missing Paws—they hunt for all pets, not just four-footed ones. They found Captain Punch, and a parrot has to be harder than a cat."

"Where are they located?" James asked. "I've never heard of them in Deerford."

"Peoria, so it wouldn't be too far for them to take a case here. My friend thought their fee was reasonable too," Anabelle said. "You can find them on the Internet."

"I hate to think of Fern without her kitty," Candace said. "Maybe Sapphire will come strutting home, tail held high, after a little adventure."

"Don't I wish!" James said. "The trouble is, we're in a new neighborhood. She might be confused about where she lives. Or worse, something might have prevented her from coming home. I worry about cars even though the traffic on our street isn't heavy."

"I didn't know there was such a thing as a pet detective," Candace said. "I thought it was only a comic movie idea. One of Brooke's friends wanted her to come over and watch one on a DVD, but she didn't go. It sounded like it had some questionable material, so I was glad Brooke didn't think she'd like it. Of course, that was several years ago. Now she pretty much wants to do anything her friends suggest. She makes me feel like a mean mother when I say no to anything."

"Someday Brooke will have children of her own, and she'll understand how hard it is to be the grown-up," Anabelle said.

Candace smiled and nodded her head. "You're right, of course. I'm not in a hurry to get old, but I can see the upside of having children outgrow the teen years. I'll miss Brooke terribly when she's old enough to be on her own, but it would be wonderful to have her as a friend."

"It will happen," Anabelle assured her. "You know how hard it's been for me to adjust to having adult children—no longer under my wing—but I've grown to love it."

"You have a lovely family," Candace said. "I hope my children grow up to be as nice as yours."

"With you as their mother, they almost certainly will," Anabelle assured her.

James was late getting home after work, thanks to a long meeting on hospital procedures. He was optimistic about his committee, especially Dr. Weller. The young physician had a lot of good ideas, but he didn't try to dominate the proceedings. But if James had learned one thing, it was how complicated emergency procedures could be. Every person on the staff from the CEO to the custodians had to be aware of their responsibilities. There couldn't be any exceptions or slipups if they faced an epidemic.

In spite of a successful day, James couldn't keep his mind off Fern's missing cat. He walked into the house with his fingers crossed, silly as that seemed to him, because it wasn't just Fern who was hoping to find their pet. The boys would get a big confidence boost if their efforts were successful. Fern would be greatly relieved to get Sapphire back, but she would also be touched by all that her sons were doing to help.

She was in the kitchen chopping vegetables for a salad, standing by the sink instead of sitting on her high stool, an indication that her MS wasn't bothering her as much today as it sometimes did. She smiled at him, but it wasn't her usual radiant grin when she was feeling well.

"Something smells good," he said.

"Spaghetti sauce. The boys have been working so hard trying to find Sapphire. I wanted to fix something they really like. I haven't started the noodles yet."

James knew that lifting a heavy kettle of water onto the stove was too taxing for her; so he automatically found the pasta pot, filled it with hot water, and put it on the stove to boil.

Gideon came home first, and James could read defeat on his face.

"I think that cat has disappeared from the face of the earth," he said glumly.

James wanted to say something encouraging, but he was losing hope too.

"She's such a beautiful animal," Fern said. "Certainly someone has taken her to the shelter. Or possibly adopted her, thinking she was a stray."

Her husband didn't want to throw cold water on her spark of optimism, but he'd already checked with the Bureau County Animal Shelter. They didn't have a cat even remotely resembling Sapphire; but an acquaintance who worked there—Josh Johnston—had promised to call if one came in.

Nelson came into the kitchen looking as downcast as his brother.

"We've put the fliers everywhere in town. Do you think it would help if the Scouts made some big posters? Maybe people aren't noticing those small sheets of paper," he said.

"It's something to keep in mind," James said tactfully. "Actually, Anabelle Scott gave me a good idea at lunch today. There's a company called Missing Paws in Peoria. A friend of hers had good luck hiring them to find a lost parrot. I thought we might give them a call if Sapphire doesn't turn up soon."

"You mean there really is such a thing as a pet detective?" Fern asked.

"Absolutely," James said.

"Cool!" Nelson said. "A real detective!"

"Apparently," James said with a smile.

"I don't know what a stranger could do that we haven't already tried," Gideon said morosely.

"I wonder whether they're terribly expensive." Fern frowned, and James knew it bothered her that she wasn't able to contribute to the family's income, especially when their old house still hadn't sold.

"We'll worry about it when the time comes," James said. "There hasn't been time for someone to see a flier and connect it to a stray cat. Even as we speak, Sapphire could be living high on tuna and milk while the person who found her wonders what to do with her."

Fern gave him a wan smile. His forced optimism wasn't fooling her.

"Now, who's hungry for spaghetti?" James asked, peering into the pot to see if it was time to dump the noodles into the water. "Your mother made the sauce, so you know it will be good."

Nelson mustered some enthusiasm, but Gideon still looked grim. No doubt his older son knew that the chances of finding Sapphire were slimming by the minute. James wasn't optimistic either, but at least Anabelle's suggestion was one more thing they could try.

Chapter Five

ANABELLE DROVE HOME AFTER WORK IN A disturbed frame of mind after running several errands. As a nurse supervisor in the Cardiac Care Unit, she was acutely aware of ailments that could affect a man her husband's age. In fact, maybe she knew too much for her own peace of mind.

When Cameron was still working in his landscaping business, he'd automatically kept fit and trim. Now, though, he'd turned the running of the business over to their son Evan and took things easier. He'd worked hard all his life, starting his business from scratch by mowing lawns, and Anabelle thought he deserved a more leisurely life. At sixty-five, he was only a year older than she was; and, at first, he'd delighted in doing things he'd never had time to do while working. He traced his Scots ancestors back eleven generations and enjoyed reading about the history of Scotland. He was teaching himself to cook and sometimes made a delicious dinner for the two of them. He never had to say no to church or community activities for lack of time, and, of course, he greatly enjoyed their first grandchild Lindsay Belle whose first birthday they would celebrate in April.

Was Cam happy with his retirement lifestyle? Was he keeping healthy without the hard exercise he used to get in his business? Should she retire to keep him company? Anabelle loved her job and wasn't ready to quit, but she couldn't shake a nagging little doubt. Maybe her place was at home with her husband.

She didn't often dwell on this thought. In fact, Cam encouraged her to keep working as long as she liked.

"It's only because he's being so secretive about his doctor," she said to herself as she pulled up in front of their boxy three-bedroom farmhouse on the edge of town.

Usually she took a minute to enjoy the view from the front of the house. They owned two pastures and a small barn in a lovely rural setting that was only two miles from the hospital. Today she was much too eager to hear about her husband's appointment to linger outside even though there was a faint promise of spring in the air, so she pulled into the garage and hit the button to close the door against the beauty outside.

Sarge met her inside the door of the mudroom.

"Hey, boy, how was your day?" she asked, petting his head as his big paws clattered on the tile floor.

What she'd said to Candace about learning to love children when they were babies certainly applied to Sarge. He'd been an adorable brown-and-white puppy with oversized paws and a whiplike tail when they found him at the shelter. It had been love at first sight when he was ten weeks old. Now he was close to the canine equivalent of a teenager, with legs, tongue, and tail in frantic motion as he panted his welcome. And she now enjoyed him even more than before.

"Sit, Sarge," Cam said, coming up behind the dog.

Her husband and Sarge had gone to obedience school together, and Cameron still called on their lessons to calm the rambunctious dog.

He took her coat while Sarge sat panting for release from the command.

"How was your day?" Cam asked, kissing her cheek before he hung the coat in the closet.

"Pretty good. I recommended Missing Paws to James. Fern's cat has disappeared."

"That's a shame, although I wouldn't mind if a few of our barn cats went missing. I think that big black-and-white male enjoys tormenting Sarge."

"The cats were here before we were—at least their ancestors were," Anabelle reminded him.

Although they didn't keep a cat in the house, they recognized the value of having some good mousers in the barn. Anabelle didn't like to think of all the little critters that would take up residence if the cats didn't stand guard.

"Well," she began, trying to sound casual, "what did you learn at the doctor's?"

"Nothing much. I gained six pounds."

"Okay..." Should she be worried? "What else?" She was resigned to coaxing information from him.

"He sliced off that wart that was bothering you." He held up his bandaged finger for inspection.

"What about your vital organs, heart, lungs, liver?"

"Oh yeah, I have to go in for a blood test before breakfast one of these days."

"Is that all?"

"Annie, lass, it was only a routine checkup." He spoke with his version of a Scottish accent, a sure sign that he was trying to kid her. "Anyway, I have a surprise for you."

"Really? A nice surprise?" She arched her eyebrows, willing to play his game.

"What's your favorite place to eat?"

"I really like that German restaurant in Peoria. It must be over a year since we went there."

"I was thinking of somewhere in Deerford." He sounded a tad disappointed that she hadn't mentioned the one he had in mind.

"Well, you can't beat the food at Heritage House. I love the idea that Abraham Lincoln once ate there when it was a private home and he was a young lawyer."

"Well, whether he did or not," Cameron said a bit skeptically, "it's the only place in the county that serves beef Wellington."

"A good Scotsman like you wants to eat a dish named after the British hero of Waterloo?" she teased.

"There's some doubt about where it got the name. I looked it up online, and the dish may have been named after boots called Wellingtons. It's sort of shaped like a foot."

"That doesn't make my mouth water. Anyway, it's Friday. There's almost no chance of a table at the Heritage House on their busiest night."

"Ah, that's my surprise. I called ahead and reserved a table for two. We'll have to go early, but you have time to spiff up before we leave."

He grinned, looking so pleased with himself that she didn't have the heart to refuse, never mind that she'd been looking forward to a quiet evening after a hectic week at work.

"I'll go get ready," she said.

"Why don't you wear your turquoise dress?" he suggested.

She paused on her way upstairs, rather surprised that Cameron had suggested a dressy jersey dress that she usually saved for special occasions.

"I like seeing you in something nicer than hospital scrubs," he said with a grin.

She didn't always wear scrubs. In fact, as a nurse supervisor she usually wore a lab coat over business-casual clothes, but she understood what he meant. The sweats she wore after work were hardly an improvement on the cotton scrubs she sometimes wore.

"If you say so," she said and offered him a flirtatious smile.

But the wife in her wondered what he was up to. Was he softening her up for bad news from the doctor?

He gave her a happy grin, reminding her of the young man she'd married. They'd been high school sweethearts, and she thanked the Lord that their love had endured so many years. She didn't know what she would do without him. That was why she worried about his doctor's appointment, especially when he was being a little too casual about the results.

Cam did have a gift for making her feel special. An hour later they were seated in a small room at one of three tables set with gleaming white linen and sparkling crystal glassware. Because it was still early, they were the first diners in the room. When the owners converted the old house into a restaurant, they'd kept as much of the original ambiance as possible, including a virtual warren of small rooms.

Their young server was smartly dressed in a burgundy jacket and black pants. He gave them small menu cards printed on linen-finish paper and asked if they would like appetizers. Anabelle was surprised when Cam immediately ordered the house special, a tray that included fried zucchini, stuffed ravioli, and breaded cheese sticks.

"We could make a meal on this," she said when it came.

Her husband filled a small plate with an assortment of goodies, but she was content to nibble on the zucchini.

"How often do we have such delicious food?" he asked between bites of cheese stick.

"We eat quite well at home," she said, meaning it as a compliment to his cooking.

He smiled between bites but didn't answer.

Their server came back after they'd enjoyed the appetizers for a few minutes.

"May I take your order now?" he asked.

Anabelle was tempted to tell him that the appetizers would do them nicely, but she would feel a little odd if she didn't order a meal in such a nice place.

"What would you like?" Cameron asked.

He always liked to order for her in restaurants, a courtesy from long ago when they'd been dating.

"The trout, please, with fresh asparagus. I'll pass on the rice pilaf."

"Oh, you might as well get it," Cam said. "You know I won't let it go to waste."

He ordered for her and requested the beef Wellington for himself along with vinaigrette for her salad and blue cheese dressing on his.

She'd forgotten one specialty of the house: a round loaf of freshly baked Italian bread, brought to the table on a wooden cutting board. Cam did the honors, slicing off thick pieces for both of them and liberally spreading his with butter and blackberry jam.

"I wonder if we could get bread this good from a bread machine," he mused after several bites. "I'm thinking of getting one like Ainslee has. Remember when we ate at her house last month?"

He sliced another piece for himself, but Anabelle declined seconds. She'd only eaten part of her bread, and she found her appetite waning. When had Cam become such a voracious eater? Was it only because the food here was especially tempting, or had his eating habits changed since retirement? He'd always enjoyed a good dinner; but, of course, when he was active all day in his landscaping business, he burned up calories too fast to gain weight. She supposed that a six-pound gain in six months wasn't horrible, but was it the beginning of an alarming trend?

She didn't say anything when he devoured the rest of the loaf along with a salad loaded with slices of hard-boiled egg, croutons, bacon bits, and thick dressing. She kept quiet when he ate every bite of the beef Wellington—medium rare tenderloin covered with beautifully browned puff pastry—and the cottage fries he'd ordered with it. When the server asked if she wanted a take-home container for the rice Cam hadn't transferred to his plate, she declined. She also passed on a choice from the luscious assortment of cakes and pies on a dessert cart wheeled to their table. Cameron looked longingly at a huge piece of carrot cake with cream cheese icing and then looked at her frowning face and decided against a sweet finish to the meal.

"That was quite a meal," he said as they walked out to their car.

"Quite a meal," she echoed, wondering what she could do about her husband's unusually huge—and unhealthy—appetite.

She'd been married too long to expect to change him, but she was deeply worried about his eating habits. Was retirement so unfulfilling that he needed to compensate with food? He didn't seem unhappy with his new routine or the amount of leisure time, but maybe she'd been too busy to notice. Their big evening out left her puzzled and worried.

Anabelle awoke several times that night, her sleep disturbed because Cam had left their room.

"Just getting an antacid," he explained when he came back the second time. "Guess I'm paying a price for the great dinner."

"We need to talk about that," she murmured, but she was much too sleepy to start that conversation in the middle of the night.

In the morning, Cam was his usual self, beating her to the kitchen and pouring out a modest portion of bran flakes for himself.

"I have a few errands to do," he said as she joined him at the breakfast bar.

"If you're going into town, wait until I get off work. I'd like to go too. I need a few toiletries at the drugstore." She sipped coffee and thought about making herself some toast.

"I'm going there. If you like, I can pick up the things you need," he offered.

"No, I like to do my own shopping. I always think of something else I can use when I wander down the aisles."

"If you're sure—I just thought you might like to have me do all the shopping."

"Don't you want me to come with you?" His unusual behavior last night had left her a little skeptical.

"Of course I do. But I plan to stop in at the company and see what Evan has on order. You know how much I enjoy it when the spring shipments come. My fingers itch to start planting."

"I wouldn't mind saying hello to our son," she assured him. "Once it gets warmer, he'll be too busy to visit with his parents." She was mostly teasing, but she did miss their son when he got especially busy.

After her shift, they went together to Peterson's Pharmacy. Anabelle went to the cosmetics area to look for her favorite moisturizer and bath powder.

"I'll meet you at the front," her husband said.

She nodded but noticed that he headed toward the back of the store and the prescription counter. There was something he wasn't telling her, but she decided to wait until they were out of the store to quiz him.

"I guess you saw me pick up some medicine," he said a bit sheepishly when they were back in the car.

"Yep. Do you want to tell me what it is?"

He sighed. "My blood pressure was a little high at the doctor's. I'm supposed to take one of these pills every day." He handed her the white paper sack that contained his prescription.

"Why didn't you tell me yesterday?" She didn't know whether to feel hurt or angry. It wasn't at all like her husband to keep secrets.

"I wanted to have a memorable meal before I start watching what I eat. The doctor said I'd have to make some changes in my diet. I guess you could call it my last supper."

"Oh, Cam." She was exasperated, concerned, and compassionate, all at the same time.

He started the engine but didn't pull out of the parking lot.

"I guess you're mad at me for not telling you. If I had, you probably wouldn't have gone to the Heritage House."

"I would have," she said thoughtfully. "Only I would have urged you to order sensibly."

"I'm not crazy about the trout you ordered. I had beef Wellington in mind."

"You could have had it as a treat without all the extras."

"I was up half the night with a stomachache, so I guess I paid the price," he grumbled.

"You know that prescription alone won't solve the problem," she said, staring at the pill bottle.

"I just assume it's not unusual for people my age to have high blood pressure. It's not that serious."

She sighed, knowing that the worst thing he could do was deny that he had a real problem.

"We'll work on it together," she said, forcing herself to sound cheerful.

"We always do," he said, reaching over and patting her hand.

She covered his hand with hers, affirming the partnership they'd shared for many years, but her mind was buzzing with questions. As a nurse, she knew that high blood pressure could be dangerous, but it was quite another thing to live with a loved one who had to control his. How would Cam's diet have to change? What about exercise? Was he getting enough? In Illinois it was often hard to even walk outside in the winter.

She pulled her hands away and sank back on the seat. This was going to be a challenge, but she dearly loved her husband. She would do whatever she could to help him.

Chapter Six

CANDACE GLANCED AT HER WATCH AND WAS surprised to see that it was only a little after ten o'clock. For some reason, the Saturday shift always seemed longer than those during the week. Maybe it was because she knew her children were home from school and there were things she could be doing with them. Fortunately, she'd changed her schedule to work Monday through Friday, but today was the exception. She'd changed with a nurse who wanted to attend her sister's wedding.

They hadn't had a single new admission in the Birthing Unit since yesterday morning, which was fairly unusual. Riley Hohmann, the nurse supervisor on her shift, had given Candace the job of taking inventory in a supply cabinet, but it wasn't a job that made time go quickly. She was happy for the diversion when she heard a commotion at the nurses' station and went to see what was happening.

"I don't feel well at all," a young woman wailed. "I'm afraid my baby's coming."

"Did your doctor tell you to come directly here?" Riley asked, frowning because the patient hadn't followed the usual procedure for checking in.

"No, I decided," her husband said, nervously shifting from one foot to the other.

He was a husky young man with a reddish complexion and thin, light-colored hair and eyebrows. He'd pushed his wife there in a wheelchair and was hovering over her.

"Have you called your doctor?" Riley asked patiently.

"All I got was her answering service. I left a message for her to meet us here. I didn't wait for them to find her. Who knows when she'd call us back," the husband said.

"I'm sure she would have responded very quickly. Are you having contractions?" the nurse supervisor asked the woman.

"She's hot all over," the husband said without giving his wife a chance to answer. "Weak and sick feeling. The baby is due in a couple of weeks, but she has stomach pains. We don't want to take any chances. Aren't you going to take her to a room or something?"

"I really don't feel well," the woman said.

"What's your name?" Riley asked.

"Lance and Nadine Bronson. This is our second kid," he said impatiently.

"And your doctor's name?"

"Dr. Carpenter."

"She lives a couple of blocks from the hospital, so she should be here soon," Riley said. "I'll give her a call to see if she's on the way. Meanwhile, Nurse Crenshaw will check your temperature and pulse."

Candace had a bad feeling about this woman. She certainly was far along in her pregnancy, but she didn't seem like a woman ready to give birth.

When Riley got off the phone, Candace motioned her aside and gave her the bad news.

"Her temp is one hundred and two."

"I suspected as much. You'd better get her down to emergency."

Candace pushed the wheelchair over the husband's protests. If this woman had the flu, the first concern was to isolate her from the patients and babies in the Birthing Unit. Fortunately the elevator was empty, and she was able to get the woman to the ER without contact with anyone else.

Dr. Weller immediately sized up the situation and took the patient to an isolated cubicle. Candace didn't know how far the committee working on emergency procedures had progressed, but the young doctor obviously took this woman's fever seriously.

"What's going on?" her husband demanded to know. "My wife could be having a baby any time now."

"Your wife is ill," the doctor said, focusing his attention on the patient. "She's not going to deliver any time soon."

Candace knew she wasn't needed, but she waited a few minutes and followed Dr. Weller when he left the cubicle. Riley would want to know his diagnosis.

"It looks like we may have our first flu patient," the doctor said with a worried frown. "I'm going to admit her for tests and isolate her until we're sure. It's bad news that she's nearly nine months pregnant."

Riley was anxiously waiting when Candace got back to her unit.

"Dr. Weller says it looks like flu. The lab will have to determine whether it's the strain we're worried about."

"I've already scrubbed and changed clothes," the nurse supervisor said. "I'll cover for you while you do the same. If the baby comes before the mother gets a clean bill of health, Dr. Carpenter will handle it without our help. This is my worst nightmare—the possibility of an epidemic in our unit."

Candace agreed. She fervently prayed that the mothers and babies in their care wouldn't be infected.

Before this, she'd thoroughly approved of the task force and the efforts to be prepared, but now the threat seemed real for the first time. Candace saw how easy it had been for a sick person to evade the usual registration procedures. How many people had the patient met in the lobby or elevator? Did her husband have the virus too? Would he spread it to others where he worked? This wasn't the Bronsons' first child. Would flu go through their family? What about their babysitter, the person who was watching their other child? She shuddered at the prospect of one sick woman starting an epidemic.

She wanted to skip her lunch and stay with their patients, as though she could somehow protect them by being there. Riley insisted she take her break, so she went down to the cafeteria, cautiously eyeing everyone she saw on the way.

One feverish patient doesn't mean an epidemic, she told herself. The flu was spread by coughs, sneezes, and contaminated surfaces. Children were especially vulnerable if they didn't have good habits like regular hand washing and not putting things in their mouths. She was probably being a little paranoid, but Candace could easily imagine the consequences if one sick person was allowed to spread the virus.

The cafeteria line was short, and she quickly chose a sandwich wrapped in plastic without paying attention to the filling. *What if someone on the kitchen staff is infected?* she thought as she added a can of soda to her tray.

Of course, everyone who worked at the hospital had been inoculated. She was worrying way too much. Ever since she'd lost her husband so suddenly nearly five years ago, she'd been overly sensitive about the closeness of death. Dean had only been thirty-six when a brain aneurysm ended his life.

Fortunately mothers rarely died in childbirth in the twenty-first century, and the Birthing Unit was usually a happy place where the staff welcomed new life into the world. She didn't know whether she could continue nursing if she had to take care of terminal patients, although she greatly admired those who did.

After she paid for her skimpy lunch, she was tempted to save it for later and return to the unit, but she caught sight of one of her favorite people waving at her to join him.

Heath Carlson was a radiologist, specializing in MRI technology. The same age as Candace, he'd suffered a tragedy when his fiancée had been killed by a drunk driver many years ago. He understood, perhaps better than anyone she knew, how devastating it was to lose a loved one. They'd become close friends because of this bond. Soon she realized how much she enjoyed his company, and after several months of dating, they had fallen in love.

He smiled, showing deep dimples in both cheeks, when she sat down across from him. His curly golden-blond hair was cut short, and he had vivid blue eyes and an easy smile. Candace admired how fit and trim he kept himself. He inspired her to exercise regularly, and fortunately she enjoyed healthy activities.

"I'm surprised to see you here on a Saturday," she said as her cheeks filled with warmth.

"I'm covering for a tech who wanted time off because his mother in Omaha is sick." He held on to her hand on the table. "So far things have been pretty quiet. How are things in the baby department?"

"We haven't had a new admission since yesterday morning," she said, wondering whether to say anything about the flu patient.

Before she could make up her mind, he began to speak.

"I'm thinking of taking time off to go to Nebraska."

"Oh? Why Nebraska?"

"There's a place off interstate 80 near Kearney where sandhill cranes go to feed in early spring on their migration north," he said, lighting up at one of his favorite subjects. "Hundreds of thousands stop there by the Platte River because it's shallow. They feed for days on remains in the cornfields before they continue on to Canada. Some even go as far as Siberia."

"That sounds incredible," she said, genuinely interested.

Since she'd gotten to know Heath, she'd become fascinated by birds, even going with him to watch them in the woods outside of town. Brooke hadn't shown much interest in the feathered creatures, but Howie was a convert, bringing home bird books from his elementary school library and putting out sunflower seeds to attract them to the bird feeder in their backyard.

"The way to see them is to reserve a place in a blind and watch at night as they return to the river. They sleep in shallow water because if a predator tries to attack them, they splash to sound a warning. It's pretty dramatic when the flocks fly. I've never seen it, so I'm hoping to get there around the twenty-third or twenty-fourth of this month. That's the soonest I can get away, but I'll still get to see some cranes according to the latest updates on the Internet. It's a really big deal for bird lovers."

"It sounds exciting."

"You could go with me."

"I'd love to, but I have to be here for Brooke's birthday party."

"We could take the kids with us," he suggested.

"Brooke? I don't think so."

They both laughed at the thought of Brooke huddled in a bird blind watching cranes. "Howie seems to like birds," he said.

"Yes, but I'm afraid his attention span is too short for bird-watching. Anyway, I can't ask my mother to stay home alone with Brooke and be in charge of the birthday celebration. My daughter is acting like a teen already, even though she won't be thirteen until the twenty-third. In fact, the plans for her birthday party are giving me fits. If I canceled it to go bird-watching, she'd never forgive me."

"That's a shame. Tell you what I'll do. I'll photograph everything I see, and we'll have a bird night with the kids after I get home. That's if I decide to go. It won't be as much fun if you can't go."

She smiled and remembered the sandwich on her tray. It turned out to be ham salad, a cafeteria special that was really ground-up bologna with pickles and mayonnaise. She took a bite. Heath had restored her appetite.

"There is one thing I would like to share with you," she said after they finished lunch and were walking out of the cafeteria together. "We had a woman come to the Birthing Unit with flu symptoms. The lab will have to determine whether it's the kind we've been warned about."

"That is bad," he said. "I'll keep quiet about it and hope it's a false alarm."

"Please do. I wouldn't want to start a panic. We haven't even had our first preparedness drill." They parted at the elevator. Grateful as she was that she'd shared her break with Heath, she couldn't shake the nagging worry that the epidemic might have started.

Candace went right home after work. She had a few errands that needed doing, but it was more important to see what her kids were up to. At sixty-one, her mother Janet Fuller had more energy than most younger women, but Candace didn't like to take advantage of her.

She stepped inside the door and found Brooke waiting for her.

"Mother, I thought you'd never get here."

Mother instead of *Mommy* was never a good sign.

"I usually get home at this time," she responded mildly. "What's up?"

"We have to talk about my birthday party."

"Just let me take my coat off and tell Grammy I'm home."

"I've been waiting hours for you to get here," her daughter said, virtually dancing around her as she hung her coat in the closet.

"Well, I'm home now. Is this a private conversation? We could go upstairs to my bedroom."

"I don't care whether Howie hears, and Grammy already knows."

"Knows what?"

"What I'd like to do for my birthday party." Brooke made no move to the stairs leading to the upper level and their bedrooms, instead planting herself in front of her mother in a challenging position.

"The plans are all made," Candace said, at a loss to see where this conversation was going. "We've reserved the social room at the Y for Saturday night. They close to the public at eight, so we'll play some games and have pizza and cake first. Then your girlfriends are welcome to use any of the facilities there."

"Mother, that's like gym class! I want a real party."

"What do you consider a *real* party? Tell me what you have in mind."

"I want to invite boys to my party."

Candace shook her head, but Brooke didn't give her a chance to protest.

"We can have music and dancing. That's what friends my age want. Tiffany is going to invite boys when she has her birthday in May."

"Brooke, you'll only be thirteen. I really think you're a little young to have a party with boys. I'm sure you can have a lot of fun with your girlfriends."

"Some fun!" Sarcasm was a new thing for Brooke. Candace did *not* like it. "Eat cake, shoot baskets in the gym, and go home. My friends won't even want to come."

"I'm sure you're exaggerating, sweetie." The endearment didn't match her daughter's attitude, but perhaps it would remind Brooke what a sweetie she was at heart and turn her attitude around. "Remember, you especially wanted to have it at the Y because you had so much fun when Carla had a party there?" Candace prompted, trying to deal calmly with her daughter's anger.

"Just because we have it there doesn't mean I want the same kind of party. Carla was only twelve then. Next you'll want us to wear silly paper hats and play baby games," Brooke said. "I don't know why you can't just think about it instead of saying no right away. I don't know what's so wrong about inviting boys."

"Why don't you go upstairs for now, and we'll talk more later."

"You're sending me to my room for asking a simple question?"

"No, I'm just suggesting that you're too upset to talk about it now."

"Like you'll change your mind later!" Brooke stomped off, still looking small and vulnerable. She'd taken her father's death very hard, not even speaking for two months. Now, after helpful counseling and the passage of time, her heart had mended. She was still very much the pretty blonde-haired, blue-eyed daughter that Dean had adored; but her mood swings sometimes taxed her mother's patience.

Candace watched her, feeling deflated and ineffective. When had her adorable little girl turned into a hostile adolescent? For a split second, a flash of grief for Dean came over her. He always had a gift for making Brooke laugh and forget her anger when something upset her. What would he do about a party with boys? She doubted that he would approve, but he would know how to say no without provoking their daughter's anger.

"Ah, I thought I heard you come home," her mother said, coming up from the lower level of the house. "I just hand-washed Brooke's pink sweater and laid it out on a towel downstairs. I hope it will dry so she can wear it to church tomorrow. She especially wants to."

"If not, she has other sweaters just as nice."

"Yes, but you know how children are when they hit the teens." Janet smiled. "Every little setback is a major tragedy."

"Were Susan and I hard to get along with then?"

"Well, your sister was three years older, so she was over her adolescent moodiness by the time you hit your teens. But I have to admit, you were always pretty even-tempered."

"Brooke wants boys at her birthday party. I'm not sure that I'm ready to handle a mixed group. She's in such a hurry to grow up."

"Children do seem to grow up faster than when I was a girl," Janet mused. "I guess each generation has to find its own way, but sometimes I think things were easier then. We didn't have so many organized activities, but we were pretty good at finding fun on our own."

"Do you think I should let her have boys at the party?"

"That's a decision you'll have to make," her mother said with a smile. "I'm glad I don't have to decide."

Chapter Seven

ELENA WATCHED HER GRANDDAUGHTER PREEN IN front of the full-length mirror. She loved to dress up, and this morning she was wearing her second-best Sunday school outfit, an emerald green jumper with a white knit top and white tights. It looked special with a long strand of green, yellow, and white beads that her father had given her. Izzy always took special pleasure in any gift from Rafael.

"I hope that bad boy doesn't break my necklace," she said.

"I'm sure he won't," Elena assured her, although there was a little rascal in her Sunday school class who seemed to delight in teasing Izzy.

"He'd better not. I'll tell him he'd better watch out because Grandfather is a policeman."

Elena had to smile. Izzy was going through a phase where she carefully pronounced *grandfather*, instead of calling Cesar by her toddler name for him, *Tito*, short for the Spanish word for grandfather. Some days she also insisted on being called Isabel, although Cesar liked to tease her by calling her Miss Isabel.

Izzy brought sunshine and happiness into their home. Even though Elena had been heartbroken when Sarah deserted Rafael and their baby—which, she realized, now felt like ages ago—she knew how blessed she had been to be able to watch her granddaughter grow up. At six—or six and a half as Isabel sometimes corrected her elders—she was a beautiful miniature woman with waist-length, curly black hair that she didn't want to cut. Her delicate features were dominated by striking gray eyes and a ready smile.

Elena wondered if Rosa Acuna was anywhere near as beautiful as Izzy. Maria had shown Elena a photograph of Rosa when she'd handed over the pile of dress pattern pieces. Rosa had a warm smile and long dark hair, but it was hard to tell much from a small picture. Elena had her measurements, and fortunately she knew a woman who had a dress form that could be adjusted to use in fitting the gown.

Cesar, as Elena expected, had been full of questions when he learned of Elena's plans to help Maria sew the dress, most of which involved whether she had time to make another commitment. He understood why she'd taken it on, but he wasn't happy about it.

"I'm ready, *Buela*," Izzy said, still calling her by a shortened form of the Spanish word for grandmother. Elena didn't even want to think that there would come a time when Izzy felt too grown-up for the endearment.

"Okay, let's get our coats," she said shooing her granddaughter ahead of her. "Be quiet now. Daddy's still sleeping."

Rafael's band had played late into the night, but Elena knew that he probably wouldn't have gone with them to church even if he'd gotten to bed early. Cesar, too, seldom went to church. Meanwhile, she took Izzy to Sunday school, delighted in the interest she showed in Bible stories.

"Do I have to go to church?" Izzy asked when they were in the car.

Some Sundays she was happy to sit through the service at Holy Trinity that followed Sunday school, but Elena didn't pressure her. She wanted her granddaughter to love church, not see the service as an ordeal. Fortunately there was time to drive her home and get back in time.

Izzy was old enough to be dropped off at the entrance to the Sunday school wing at the back of the church, but most Sundays Elena liked to walk to the classroom with her. She liked seeing what the lesson was, and she enjoyed the colorful child-friendly room with low tables and chairs. Her granddaughter was still too young to object to being escorted there, and she held Elena's hand and happily chatted while they walked into the building.

Elena waited while Izzy hung her bright pink winter jacket on a low rack in the hallway and went into the classroom. She was going to leave then, but a large poster on the bulletin board caught her eye. The church offered classes from time to time, and the theme of the new series sounded particularly worthwhile: The Call to Follow. Unlike her Wednesday night Bible class which met throughout the year, the new classes would only run for ten weeks. They were open to all members of the congregation, while the Wednesday classes were usually attended by women only.

Although she usually went to Sunday school herself, she decided to go home instead this morning. Izzy would be perfectly all right, and she could get back well before her class was over. She hadn't seen her husband nearly enough lately.

A few minutes later she was seated across the kitchen table from Cesar. There was something comforting about seeing her husband in his pajamas and dark red robe. Time had been kind to him. As a mature adult approaching fifty, he was even more attractive than the young man she'd married. Like all marriages, theirs had had its ups and downs, but she couldn't imagine life without him.

It was a concern for Elena that Rafael didn't yet have the kind of stable relationship that his parents did. He was as handsome as his father, with eyes so dark they seemed to be black and black hair that framed a fine-boned and pleasing face. Certainly young women were attracted to him. He always seemed to find girlfriends, including a short romance with the band's backup singer, but he didn't seem ready for commitment.

Elena never doubted that her son had been deeply in love with Sarah. Even after she deserted him, he kept alive the hope that she would beat her addiction and return to him. But years passed and he couldn't hide his disappointment from his mother. Fortunately his newfound interest in becoming a police officer like his father had lifted his spirits and given him an incentive to excel in his community college classes.

Cesar had made a fried egg and charred toast for his breakfast. They often joked that cooking his own breakfast was his penance for not going to church, but Elena scarcely noticed the remains on his plate this morning.

"What's on your mind?" he asked, too well attuned to her moods to ignore the look on her face.

"There's something I'd really like to do."

Cesar was quiet for a moment, drumming his fingers on the tabletop.

"Well, are you going to tell me?" he asked with a trace of impatience.

"Pastor Flynn is offering a new class at church. It looks especially interesting."

"You already go to Bible study every Wednesday evening."

"This is different. It only runs for ten sessions on Sunday evenings. It's a great chance to explore the reason for following the Lord."

"Sunday evening? That's the one night we usually have to ourselves."

"You could go with me," Elena suggested.

He sighed and rolled his eyes—not a good sign.

"It's only an hour or so. You might actually like going." Elena greatly regretted that Cesar didn't share her recently rediscovered faith. She hung on to the hope that someday he would hear the Word of the Lord and believe, but she knew from experience that it wouldn't help to push him. "Will you think about it?"

"I suppose."

He got up to clear his place at the table, and Elena said a silent prayer that the class wouldn't become an issue between them. It was something she really wanted to do.

After church the day went quietly. When Cesar was upset, he busied himself with household chores and avoided Elena. She was glad that he changed the furnace filter and installed the new showerhead that they'd bought several weeks ago, but she was a person who liked to talk through issues. Still, she knew it was best to keep silent until he was in a better mood.

She reluctantly put aside the spring dress she was making for Izzy and turned her attention to the box of dress pieces Mrs. Acuna had given her. The tissue paper pattern was still pinned on, and Maria had started to mark the darts with thread. Elena was glad she hadn't tried to mark the delicate fabric with dressmaker's chalk. It showed that she had the skill and patience to make a beautiful quinceañera gown. Elena hoped she could do justice to it, although it would test her skill to the limit.

She'd planned to make fried chicken for dinner, a favorite with her family, but instead she breaded the pieces and put them in the oven to bake, saving time to continue working on the dress. It hadn't taken her long to realize she would have to baste the bodice by hand and fit it on the dress dummy before attempting to sew it on the machine. The silk lining was slippery and hard to handle. Fortunately, she liked a challenge, but she didn't even want to think about how much time this project was going to take.

Chapter Eight

"I MAY BE LATE STARTING DINNER," ELENA SAID AS SHE put Cesar's breakfast in front of him Monday morning. "The task force is meeting again when my shift ends."

"How's that coming?" he asked, spearing one of the little sausages on his plate. "Hopefully your part will be winding down soon."

"Not yet. I'll know more after today's meeting."

"So what exactly are you doing?" he asked a bit gruffly.

"I'll be doing something with communications, working with Maxine Newman, the county health nurse. She's very professional, but she's also good with people. I think Penny Risser would like to be in charge, but Maxine has a way of reining her in without putting her down."

"You have a good group working on it, don't you?" he said, his tone softening a little. "I remember you mentioned James is in charge of hospital preparedness."

"Yes, and Anabelle's working on the vaccines with Dr. Hamilton. There aren't going to be nearly enough shots for everyone who might want them if an epidemic hits. I'm glad I don't have to help decide who gets them. Candace is on the task force too."

"You've got the fabulous four working," he said in a sardonic tone. "I never expected your job to take more time than mine."

"Only temporarily," she assured him.

"Any second thoughts about taking that Sunday evening class?"

"It's only an hour or two a week for ten weeks." She didn't ask him again to join her, but they knew each other so well that sometimes words weren't necessary.

"I don't want to go," he said, "but I'll think about giving it a try—only because it looks like the only way I'll get to spend some time with my wife."

"Thank you, Cesar," she said softly.

"Just the first session—that's all I'm promising to consider."

She stood behind him and leaned around to plant a kiss on his forehead. "I have to leave," she said, dashing off before he could change his mind.

When Elena arrived at the nurses' station in ICU, she made a conscious effort to put thoughts about her busy schedule out of her mind. She firmly believed that her patients deserved her full attention. Anything less was unprofessional and unfair to the seriously ill people in her charge. Her first concern was the coma patient who was still in their unit.

Gloria Main, the night nurse, filled her in on the patients but didn't mention the unidentified one.

"What about our coma patient?" Elena asked. "Any sign that she might wake up?"

"No, everything is the same as it was last Friday. We still don't have a clue who she is."

"Someone must miss her. People don't disappear without anyone noticing. Newspapers could pile up on her doorstep. Neighbors might notice that she hasn't taken her car out for days. This isn't Chicago. People in Deerford know their neighbors and look out for them."

"True," Gloria said sadly, shaking her head. "I went through her clothing again and the pockets were empty except for some tissues and a house key. Her sweats are good quality, not what you'd expect to see on a homeless person. And her shoes are expensive, maybe a hundred dollars or more."

"She doesn't look much older than fifty," Elena mused. "You would expect that she has a job if she lives on her own. Her boss should check on her if she doesn't come to work or call."

"You'd think so," Gloria said, "but the poor thing is lying there all alone. I imagine they'll move her to a long-term facility if she doesn't wake up pretty soon."

Elena drummed her fingers on the counter that surrounded the nurse supervisor's desk.

"I wish I could do something."

"I know," Gloria said sympathetically. "The worst cases are the ones where we can't do anything to help."

As soon as she had a chance, Elena looked in on their mystery patient. She looked terribly frail and helpless in her cocoon of tubes and monitors, and Elena tried to will her to wake up. It was hopeless, of course. Doctors had no idea when or if she'd ever recover consciousness.

Being alone made the woman's situation even worse. She didn't have anyone to hold her hand and talk to her. Elena was convinced, on instinct alone, that coma patients could hear what was said to them. She always carried on a one-sided conversation, regardless of whether a patient could respond.

"I'm sure someone must be missing you," she said. "It's too bad you didn't carry a cell phone. Then we could trace some of your friends. But don't worry. We have some very clever people on our police force. I know because my husband is one of them. I'm sure they'll learn something about you soon."

Before she left the room, Elena took another hard look at the patient. There was something vaguely familiar about her round, pale face. She looked like a friendly person, but, of course, that was only speculation. Her blonde hair was graying at the temples, but the mix was probably attractive when her hair was nicely shampooed and styled. In fact, she had a good haircut. Elena guessed that it had been recently cut.

"Have I seen you somewhere before?" she asked the unresponsive patient. "Where do you buy groceries? Do you have a doctor or dentist in Deerford? Do you shop at Once Upon a Time or the Chocolate Garden?" She left the room still wondering how long it would be before someone reported the woman missing. At least there wasn't any shortage of relatives waiting to hear about other patients in the ICU. They had one terminal patient and another who wasn't doing as well as expected after surgery. Visitation was strictly limited, but sometimes it broke

Elena's heart to see the anxious, tearful faces of those waiting for news.

By the end of her shift Elena felt more like taking a nap than going to a task force meeting, but it was too important to miss. She got on the elevator just as Anabelle was hurrying toward it and held the door for her friend.

"How was your day?" Elena asked.

"Busy. I know how important the task force is, but I hope the meeting doesn't last too long. I'm eager to get home to Cam. I'm a little worried about what he'll make for dinner."

"I thought he was turning into a pretty good cook. I'd love to have Cesar fix dinner, but that's not going to happen."

Anabelle smiled at Elena's feigned exasperation. "Cam does well, but he has to watch what he eats for the first time in his life. He just found out that he has high blood pressure."

Elena frowned. "That's a shame. I can't imagine Cam on a diet. He's always been so slender."

The elevator door slid open, and Elena excused herself for a moment to run into the gift shop. She wanted to get a package of grape-flavored gum for Izzy, and this was the only place she knew that sold it.

On the way out, she saw Candace coming out of the cafeteria carrying a take-out cup.

"Oh good," the petite younger woman said. "You're not at the meeting yet, so I won't be the last one. I couldn't resist picking up some iced tea on the way."

Elena touched Candace's arm. "I heard a rumor that the hospital admitted an obstetrics patient with flu symptoms. I hope it's not true."

"I'm afraid it is," Candace said with a worried expression. "Her husband ignored the registration desk and brought her right to the Birthing Unit. We sent her down to Emergency, of course, but it showed how vulnerable our patients are. I haven't heard how her tests came out. During an epidemic, I guess we'd have to close our unit to all outsiders, maybe even husbands."

"I'm sure James will come up with a comprehensive plan. My question is, will the hospital board second-guess all his recommendations? Does he have the authority to insist on preventive measures?"

"Let's hope so," Candace said.

"Let's pray we'll never have to use his plan, whether the board approves it or not."

People were still milling around in the community health room, and Maxine was talking to Penny at one end of the table. Neither of them looked happy.

"Thank you all for coming," the county nurse said after a few minutes. "I'll start by passing on some good news. No doubt most of you have heard something about an obstetrics patient admitted with flu symptoms. She does indeed have flu, but only the seasonal strain. She was sent home as soon as the report came back from the state lab."

Candace raised her hand, and Maxine recognized her with a nod.

"What will happen if she goes into labor before she gets a clean bill of health on the flu virus?"

"I think James is best qualified to answer that question," Maxine said. "His group has been working hard on an overall plan."

"Naturally we're hoping that baby will be a real slowpoke," James said, "but preparedness is all about planning for the worst scenario. If all we have to worry about is one sick OB patient, we can isolate her in the General Medicine Unit."

Dr. Weller nodded agreement, and James asked whether he would like to comment.

"No, you're doing fine," the good-natured young doctor said.

"The first thing we would have to do is cancel all optional surgery. Intensive Care, Birthing, and Cardiac Care Units would continue to receive patients under strict admission procedures."

Elena listened avidly, agreeing with almost everything he said, but she had a hard time seeing the cafeteria as an emergency ward.

"People will still need to eat," she said when James acknowledged her.

"Of course, but it's possible to isolate the kitchen from the dining area and send out food through the back entrance. Remember, this is a plan for extreme emergencies. None of us expects an epidemic that serious."

"We can save valuable time if we plan for the worst possible situation," Dr. Weller said in support of James.

Elena knew James well, and his serious demeanor was more alarming than any of his preparations. Major disasters were events on the television. She had a hard time imagining Deerford in a crisis situation, but there was comfort in knowing they had a plan.

The senior physician, Dr. Hamilton, was the next to voice his concerns.

"Here's the situation, folks," he said in an uncharacteristically grim tone. "Hope Haven now has control of all available vaccine in the county. We've decided to administer it only on the recommendations of physicians. They're in the best position to target high-risk patients. In an epidemic, we'll probably be besieged with requests, but we'll be much too busy to screen them."

The group around the table murmured approval, but Dr. Hamilton had more to say.

"That means you'll need to go through your personal physicians if family members haven't received shots yet," he warned.

No doubt that will cause some distress, Elena thought, as she pictured Rafael and his nonchalant attitude about getting a shot. There was nothing she could do for him now.

Maxine called on her last to update the task force on communications.

"Mrs. Newman is sending out e-mail notices to all area physicians updating them on the situation," Elena began.

"Don't you think they should be sent daily?" Penny asked, breaking what was for her a long silence.

"No," Elena said, steeling herself for controversy. "If we send announcements too frequently, they won't be taken seriously. It was decided to keep them short."

"Good," Dr. Hamilton said. "Keep them under a paragraph. Wordy alerts sent too often will only desensitize people. Anything that comes from the county health office should be brief and concise."

Elena appreciated support from the senior physician, but she wasn't through with her report; the skeptical look on Penny's face suggested that she wasn't through interrupting.

"We've arranged for articles in the local paper and the staff newsletter outlining the situation and what we're doing about it," Elena continued.

"You know what will happen as soon as the press gets onto this," Penny said in an ominous voice. "The hospital will be besieged with people who think they have it."

"They'll be coming in through Emergency," Dr. Weller said. "We're setting up a process to examine and treat an influx of the worried well. Most will only need reassurance, I hope. If things get too hectic, we have a retired doctor and several retired nurses who are willing to help out."

Elena finished her report with her head reeling from all the complications of handling a real epidemic.

She drove home trying to focus on what she would make for dinner, but the possibility of an epidemic was too upsetting to push it out of her mind. Even though it was still cold and overcast, March could be a pleasant month in Deerford with the promise of spring ahead. She loved it when the trees first budded and warm breezes called people outside. She never thought of it as a time when the flu was likely to hit.

She went into the kitchen and was surprised by a spicy aroma. The Crock-Pot was sitting out on the counter, and she went over to peek through the glass cover without lifting it.

"Surprise!"

Cesar, Rafael, and Izzy popped into the kitchen as though they'd been waiting for her.

"Your mother sent chili home from her restaurant with Rafael," her husband explained. "He told her how much time you were putting into the task force, and your nice mother wanted you to have a good dinner without having to cook."

"That's lovely," Elena said. "I'll call and thank her."

"After dinner is soon enough," Rafael said.

"I have another surprise for you!" Izzy said, practically dancing with excitement as she held both arms behind her back.

"Show her," Rafael urged.

Izzy grinned and shoved a folded piece of white paper in her direction.

"This is for me? Let me guess. Did someone special make a picture for me?"

"Open it!" Izzy insisted.

"Oh my!"

Elena grinned broadly as she saw what Izzy had drawn. There were four people dressed in capes and colorful outfits. It wasn't hard to tell that the biggest figure was her, with long brown hair and a red and blue costume that looked like a ballerina's. James was easy to identify, even in purple tights and a black mask. Anabelle had white hair and fire seemed to be coming from her fingers. The fourth person had to be Candace, even though Izzy had made her hair bright red instead of wavy brown with copper highlights. She was wearing blue tights and an orange top with green stripes.

"See, I put an *S* on your shirt because you're a super nurse and a super grandmother," Izzy pointed out.

"And a super mama," her son added.

"Not to mention a super wife," Cesar said, beaming at her.

"This is so lovely," Elena said, just barely holding back tears of happiness.

"It's the fabulous four," Rafael said. "Whenever Hope Haven is in trouble, you, James, Candace, and Mrs. Scott come to the rescue."

Elena laughed. "This is just... *excelente!*" Elena went to the fridge and affixed the picture with a magnet. "It's not just us, though. Everyone at the hospital does their best."

"Not like the fabulous four," her husband said, giving her a big hug.

Rafael and Izzy joined them for a group hug. She couldn't think of a better end for a hectic day.

Chapter Nine

ANABELLE HURRIED HOME AFTER THE TASK FORCE meeting. It was past their usual dinnertime, and she wondered whether Cameron had eaten without her as she'd suggested. She was famished, but there was no reason for him to wait if he was hungry.

The meeting had gone well. Everyone seemed more than willing to let local physicians screen their patients to determine who most needed the limited amount of vaccine. Unfortunately, her responsibilities didn't end there. The committee still had to set up a system for administering and recording the shots. Dr. Hamilton wanted statistics to use in case of an epidemic. He wanted to know how effective the protective measures were. She'd known him for many years and respected his cautious approach, but it would require extra hours of work to implement.

Sarge met her at the door, tongue lolling and tail wagging, but his lessons at the obedience school kept him from jumping up on her, something she appreciated because he'd ruined more than one pair of hose before his schooling.

"Well, you put in a long day," her husband said as he came into the mudroom. "You must be tired."

"You could say that," she said with a halfhearted smile. "But the task force is working hard. Everyone is taking the possibility of an epidemic very seriously. Even if we don't see a single case of the dangerous flu, we'll be better prepared for any kind of disaster."

"That's good," he said, "even though I hate to see you putting in such long hours. Anyway, I have dinner ready. I made soup because it's easy to keep warm. I had no idea when you'd get here."

She followed him into the kitchen, and Cam lifted the lid on a big pot sitting on the stove.

"I used my mother's recipe for bean soup. Made the whole thing from scratch just the way she used to."

Anabelle remembered eating her mother-in-law's soup when they were still newlyweds. His mother was a wonderful cook, but she was heavy-handed with fat and salt, two things that Cam especially needed to avoid.

He'd set the table with a pale blue linen cloth she usually reserved for special meals. While she watched, he lit two white tapered candles that he'd set on either side of a bouquet of flowers.

"Goodness, what's the occasion?" she asked.

"Don't you remember? March 7 was our first date. What better excuse for a special dinner together?"

"I didn't know you were so romantic," she said, genuinely touched because Cam had remembered that long-ago day. "We double-dated with your friend Barney. I can't remember the girl he was with."

"Neither can I, but I only had eyes for you."

"Time went so fast. It's hard to believe that we're grandparents now."

"The best is still to come," he said smiling. "Now why don't you freshen up while I bake the bread sticks? They only take thirteen minutes."

To get into the spirit of the evening, Anabelle quickly changed into a long burgundy velvet housecoat that was pretty enough to be an evening gown. Cameron had given it to her two years ago at Christmas, and she hadn't worn it nearly enough. She fluffed her short silvery hair and put on a favorite shade of lipstick and a spray of cologne. Some of her tiredness passed away as she went to join her husband for the special meal he'd prepared.

He served an appetizer course, cheese sticks breaded and deep fat fried. They came ready-made from the freezer section of the grocery store, and Anabelle enjoyed one while Cam ate a half dozen or so.

When it came time to serve the soup, he brought the pot to the table and ladled large portions into their bowls. He returned the remainder to the stove to keep warm in case they wanted seconds and brought in a platter of bread sticks swimming in garlic butter.

"I started the soup this morning, but I put the beans to soak after you went to bed last night," Cameron proudly said. "The hard part was getting a big ham bone with lots of meat on it. What do you think?"

Anabelle took one sip and then another, followed by a big gulp of water. The soup was just like his mother's: unpleasantly salty with fatty bits of ham and bacon in every bite. She broke off a piece of bread stick and put it in her mouth to avoid answering. It tasted delicious, but he'd obviously made his own garlic butter using the real thing.

"It is just like your mother's," she said.

After a few more spoons of soup, she knew that she wasn't going to be able to finish her portion. She drained the glass of water and watched in consternation as Cam finished his serving and went to the kitchen for seconds.

"Is something wrong?" he asked, noticing her uneaten portion when he returned to the table.

She didn't want to hurt his feelings, but she was too worried about his high blood pressure to keep silent.

"It's pretty salty," she commented mildly.

"I followed Mom's recipe exactly," he said a bit defensively.

"Yes, but . . . honey, that's the problem. The recipe calls for way too much salt."

"I like it this way." His good mood was dissolving.

"I know, but food this salty is the last thing you should be eating. Diet is an important part of controlling your blood pressure. That includes regulating your salt intake."

"I didn't think it would hurt, just this once. I wanted to make a good old-fashioned soup for a special dinner."

"I appreciate it. I really do, but I'm concerned about you. We both have to rethink the way we cook and eat."

"So I should feed the rest to Sarge?" he asked in a flippant tone.

"Dear, no. We agreed not to feed him table scraps."

"My soup isn't even fit for the dog," he said morosely.

"You did a great job following your mother's recipe. It's just not a dish that belongs in your diet."

"Next you'll tell me that the banana cream pudding I made for dessert isn't good for me either."

"Your mother's recipe?" Anabelle remembered that she always used ingredients like cream, butter, and lard in her desserts.

"Afraid so."

"We still have half a carton of strawberries in the fridge. I'll slice them, and you can have fresh fruit with a dollop of pudding on top. What could be a nicer treat than fresh berries in March? I still can't get used to seeing them in the market all winter. When we were young, we had to wait until summer."

Cam grudgingly ate a bowl of strawberries with a tablespoon of pudding, but Anabelle knew she'd hurt his feelings. Later she would put the leftovers in the freezer in small packets so he didn't feel his efforts were completely unappreciated. When her husband had gone upstairs to get ready for bed, she found the material that the doctor had sent home with him. The list of dos and don'ts wasn't complicated. In fact, it recommended a moderate amount of exercise, weight control, and the kind of diet that would benefit anyone. He still got a fair amount of exercise. The hard part would be convincing Cameron that he could no longer eat anything he liked.

It was unfortunate that this had happened just when he was taking an interest in cooking. Maybe she would have to go back to preparing all the meals herself, but she hated to deprive him of a new hobby when he most needed one.

Cameron got up when she did the next morning and joined her in the kitchen wearing his comfortable plaid robe. He didn't make coffee or offer to fix breakfast for her, although it had become part of his routine to do so in recent months. Anabelle knew why. He was still cross because she hadn't liked his soup.

She could lecture him about the need to cut down on salt when his blood pressure was high, but she knew it wouldn't do any good. His feelings were hurt over the soup, especially since he'd gone out of his way to make it for a special meal.

Her husband was a smart man, but he had a blind spot when it came to eating. His whole life he'd been so active that he could pretty much eat anything he wanted. Now that he was retired and had high blood pressure, things had to change.

"I suppose you want to make dinner," he said glumly.

"Why don't I stop at the store on the way home and get some nice chicken breasts? You always like them."

"Whatever," he said, using her least favorite word.

"I'll get some sweet potatoes too. You love them mashed."

"Seasoned with kosher salt and swimming in butter."

If she didn't know him so well, Anabelle might accuse him of being sarcastic. "You'd be surprised how good food tastes without a lot of seasoning, not that there aren't plenty of ways to make things delicious without salt and a lot of fat."

She checked herself. His face became blank when she started talking about alternative ways of cooking, and she knew nothing was sinking in.

"Fix whatever you like," he said with a shrug.

Anabelle's day didn't improve when she got to work. Becky, one of her nurses, had called in sick. She had no reason to believe the usually conscientious RN wasn't home ill; but as nurse supervisor of Cardiac Care and a member of the task force, she needed to know exactly what was wrong with her. If she had flu symptoms, it would raise a warning flag over the whole unit.

She called Becky's home three times before nine o'clock and got an answering machine each time. Perhaps she'd gone back to bed and hadn't wanted to be disturbed, but that didn't put Anabelle's mind at ease. After a fourth call went unanswered, she remembered that Becky's husband managed the produce department at the local supermarket. With fears of an epidemic hanging over the hospital, she felt justified in calling him at work to check on his wife's symptoms.

"Dirk," she said when she was transferred to his department, "This is Anabelle Scott at Hope Haven. I don't know whether Becky has talked to you about the possibility of a flu epidemic, but it has us all a bit edgy. Becky isn't answering her phone, so I wonder if you could tell me what her symptoms are."

"Her symptoms?" He sounded a bit dumbfounded.

"How did she seem this morning? Headache, fever, upset stomach?"

"She seemed fine to me, but I left for work before she was up. Isn't she at work?"

"No, she called in sick."

"Well, I don't understand that. She's been in a chipper mood lately."

"Maybe it's just a misunderstanding," Anabelle said, although she very much doubted that.

Becky was a reliable nurse who rarely took time off for any reason. If she had needed to do something, she could have requested a personal day without offering any explanation. Instead she'd called in sick. It didn't make sense, and Anabelle didn't like it. Her nurses dealt with life-and-death situations every day. She needed to be able to trust them without reservations.

There was no point in calling again, but she and Becky would have a very serious conversation when she came back to work.

Anabelle didn't have long to wait. Becky came into the unit before noon casually dressed in jeans and a green corduroy jacket. Her dark hair, usually worn in a ponytail, was streaming over her shoulders and her usually pale face was flushed. Anabelle first thought it was a sign of fever, but the younger nurse quickly dispelled that idea.

"I wanted you to be the first to know," Becky said. "I wasn't sick this morning. I just didn't want anyone to know where I was going until I knew for sure."

"Knew what for sure?" Anabelle wasn't quite ready to forgive her falsehood.

"I'm going to have a baby! I went to the doctor this morning, and it's certain."

"Congratulations!" Anabelle smiled and decided the big talk wasn't necessary. She understood why Becky wanted to be secretive until she was sure. "I have to tell you, you have several messages from me on your phone. I'll be checking everyone who calls in sick for flu symptoms."

"Oh, I didn't think of that," Becky said contritely. "I should have known a sick call would make you suspicious. Everyone is talking about the possibility of an epidemic."

"I wasn't suspicious," Anabelle corrected her. "I just have to take more notice of anyone who's ill. The whole idea behind the task force is to anticipate an epidemic and be prepared for it. But I'm very happy to hear your news."

"I'll be here tomorrow for sure," Becky promised. "In fact, if you need me, I can get some hospital scrubs and come to work now."

"We have a substitute. Why don't you use the rest of the day to spread the good news?"

"Thank you so much. My mother is going to be thrilled. I can't wait to tell her and everyone I know."

"Thank you for letting me know why you weren't here," Anabelle said. "Although next time, it would be better to tell me ahead of time. It would have saved me calling your home phone and your husband."

"Oh dear, did you talk to him at work? I was going to save my news for this evening, but he'll be wondering what's up. I'd better go see him right now."

Anabelle watched her hurry away. She didn't think Becky would try to keep more secrets.

After a worrisome morning both at work and at home, Anabelle wanted to get away from the hospital during her lunch break. She got her coat and walked across the street to the Diner on the Corner, a casual place that hospital staff liked to frequent when they got tired of cafeteria food.

The long, narrow restaurant was crowded. All the booths were occupied, so she glanced at the few tables to the left and was gratified to see that James was sitting alone at one. He spotted her and waved her over.

"Sit down," he invited, standing until she put her coat on one of the empty chairs and sat across from him.

"Hard morning?" he asked with enough of a twinkle in his eye to invite her confidences.

"A nurse called in sick. I tried to find out what was wrong in case she had flu symptoms. Turned out she was at the doctor's."

"Let me guess. She's expecting."

"How do you do that?"

"Just a lucky hunch," he said.

The waitress came and took her order for a tuna sub, one of her favorites. She found herself wondering whether it was a healthy choice. Fish was always good, but what about the salt in canned tuna? So many things they enjoyed as a couple had high levels of sodium. Cameron's new diet was going to be a real challenge.

"Have you found Sapphire?" she asked while they both waited for their food.

"No, and I'm worried that she's gone for good. Fern tries to keep her spirits up, but she really misses her. A cat is the perfect companion for her."

"It's such a shame. I know how attached people can get to pets."

"I did take your advice. I looked up the pet detective. Who knew people really make a living tracing lost animals?" He shook his head with a smile.

"Are they on the case?"

"Not yet, but I'm meeting with one of their detectives as soon as he—or maybe she—can get to Deerford. They're busier than I could have imagined."

"What they do is pretty unique."

"I still have no idea how they go about tracing a cat. The boys have tried everything with a lot of help from the Scouts. We didn't get a single response to the posters. Needless to say, they're pretty disappointed."

"Well, it will be interesting to hear what the pet detective suggests."

Their meals came, and Anabelle decided that her sandwich was large enough for two people. Restaurants seemed to think their portions should be large enough for a person doing heavy manual labor. Or maybe they were afraid of losing business if they didn't make their servings generous.

"Half of this sandwich would be about the right size," she said, dividing it into two parts before biting into the fresh whole-wheat bun overflowing with tuna salad, lettuce, tomato, and pickles. "I wish I had time to take the other half home to Cameron. I've no idea what he'll have for lunch—maybe the terribly salty soup he made for us last night."

"He's really into cooking, isn't he?"

"He was. I'm afraid I discouraged him. He used his mother's recipe to make bean soup, and it was everything he shouldn't be eating with high blood pressure—excessive salt and lots of fatty meat."

"I like things well salted too. I have to watch myself with the saltshaker," James admitted. "Fern is a light eater, but my boys are at the age where they can eat everything in sight and stay slim. Cooking for them tempts me. I can't eat the way I used to."

"Those days are gone forever for Cam," she said. "I don't know how I'm going to convince him to change, especially since he's home all day and I'm not."

"You probably can't," James said, sounding uncharacteristically pessimistic. "He'll have to decide for himself that he wants to be healthy and eat the way he should."

"You're right," Anabelle admitted sadly. "No matter what I fix for dinner, I can't control what he eats all day. He loves salty crackers, nuts, and chips. Even if I throw away everything in the house that he shouldn't have, he's not a child. He'll buy what he wants to eat. It hurts to admit it, but I may do more harm than good if I make a big fuss."

"Cam respects you. I'm sure he'll listen, but . . ." He shrugged. Even optimistic James couldn't be sure her husband would ever change his ways.

"Yes, he'll hear me, but that doesn't mean he'll act on what I say."

"You've always worked things out together," James reminded her. "Maybe when Cam gets used to the idea, he'll be cooperative."

"And maybe Sapphire will come home wearing magic boots and a feathered hat."

He laughed with her. She did feel better venting with James, but her problem was far from solved. Would Cam even eat the healthy meal she had planned for this evening?

Chapter Ten

*A*FTER WORK ANABELLE SPENT NEARLY AN HOUR in the supermarket, triple the time it would usually take her to pick up a few things for dinner. After reading the labels on a dozen or so salad dressings, she realized that she couldn't take anything for granted when it came to making healthy selections. She finally found a vinaigrette without any saturated fats that was lower than most in sodium content, but it occurred to her that she might do better making her own in the future.

Cam liked chicken dipped in egg then rolled in her special corn flake breading that included salt as a seasoning. That wasn't what he was getting this evening. She was going to make chicken packets, an idea she'd thought up today. Each breast would be wrapped in foil along with a chunk of sweet potato, several big button mushrooms, and pieces of onion. She bought some salt-free poultry seasoning and hoped the results would be tasty.

The ready-to-use bags of salad greens were tempting, but she studied the whole vegetables in the produce section. The romaine looked fresh, and she didn't begrudge the extra time it would take to wash and chop ingredients for a dinner salad. The tomatoes were a little winter-pale, but Cam didn't think a salad was a salad without them. Most years he grew more in his garden than they could use.

He wasn't home when she got there, but it didn't take a detective to discover what he'd eaten that day. A small frying pan with egg residue was soaking on one side of the double kitchen sink, the stovetop was sprinkled with kosher salt that had missed its target, and a bowl crusted with the remains of bean soup was on the counter.

Cam usually loaded the dishwasher and cleaned the stove and countertops. He seemed to be telling her that he would eat as he pleased, and it worried her to see him so careless about his health.

The chicken breasts were done in about forty-five minutes, but Anabelle had to turn down the oven to keep them warm for another half hour before her husband got home.

"Sorry I'm late," he said nonchalantly. "I went with Evan to look at a possible job. A guy wants to line his drive with a hedge and landscape the front of his house. I think Evan has a good chance of getting the job."

"Lucky for you our son has the business now so you can tag along."

"I like to think there's still a few things I can teach him." He sounded a bit indignant, not a good start to dinner.

"I'm sure there are," she agreed. "Evan is fortunate that you're still interested."

"I'll probably do a little part-time work for him during the busy season. Work off those extra pounds I put on during the winter."

"That's a good idea, but it will take more than that to control your blood pressure." She hadn't meant to lecture, but she knew Cameron too well. He was still in denial about the need to change his diet.

"I feel great for a man my age," he assured her. "I just need to get outside more."

"Well, dinner is probably overcooked. I didn't expect you to be this late."

"Sorry, I should have called. Let me wash up, and we can eat."

While he freshened up, she gingerly opened the chicken packets, carefully spearing the foil with a fork to let steam escape so it wouldn't burn her. The contents didn't look very appetizing. The sweet potato chunks were mushy and the mushrooms had shriveled into blackish lumps. The breasts seemed a little dry when she tested them, and the onions were definitely overcooked.

She measured the dressing for their salads and deliberately left the saltshaker in the cupboard, although she did put a wooden pepper mill in the center of the table. Cam could grind as much as he liked onto his food.

Cam asked a blessing on their meal and then looked at it with a grim expression.

"So this is a healthy dinner?" he asked in a sour voice that was totally unlike him.

"I admit the sweet potato is overcooked. You were late."

He pushed his fork into the mushy orange chunk and then noticed that both salt and margarine were missing from the table.

"All I can use is pepper?"

"I used poultry seasoning on the chicken. It might not need anything else."

He reached for the pepper mill and made a production out of turning it and liberally sprinkling his whole dinner with black granules.

"Cam, you don't like pepper that well," she said, taken aback by the amount on his food.

"I guess I'll have to learn to like it."

He passed up dessert, a fruit salad with lemon yogurt, but helped her clean the kitchen as he often did.

Anabelle planned to use the evening to catch up on small jobs like washing hose and doing her nails, but Cam convinced her to watch a documentary on television about research into the story of Moses. She was fascinated to see many aspects of the biblical story confirmed by modern-day findings, but her long day got the best of her. She dozed off before the end, and Cameron woke her.

"Time for bed," he said, turning off the television.

She started toward their bedroom but saw that he was getting the leash.

"Sarge and I both need some exercise," he said, fastening the leash to the excited dog's collar. "You go on to bed. You're the one who has to get up early."

She was too sleepy to object, even though it was early. Maybe she would have some better ideas on how to help Cam with his diet after a good night's sleep. He'd hated his dinner tonight, but there was no point in blaming him for being late. He probably wouldn't have liked it if it hadn't been overcooked.

As soon as her head hit the pillow, she nodded off, but deep sleep evaded her. Perhaps because her husband hadn't come to bed yet, she suddenly awoke and sat upright, checking the clock to see that it was only a little past eleven o'clock.

The last she'd seen of Cam, he was leaving to walk the dog. Had something happened to him? Their road didn't have much traffic, but still, he could have been hit by a car as he walked in the dark.

Propelled by worry, she slid out of bed, not even bothering to locate her slippers, and ran barefooted to the kitchen where a light was still showing.

Her fear vanished, but what she saw made her just as agitated. Cam was sitting at the table reading a book and eating a sandwich stacked so high with meat, cheese, and tomato that he could hardly get his mouth around it.

"Cameron Scott!"

"Oh, hi, Annie. I'm just having a little snack before I go to bed."

"A little snack?" She was as close to speechless as she ever got.

"That dinner wasn't very filling, you know," he said with a touch of petulance. "Fortunately I found a can of processed meat way at the back of the cupboard. Thought I might as well use it up. Remember, you used to fry it with mustard. It's not much good cold, but mayo and some pickles help."

Sarge sat beside him on his haunches, obviously begging; and she suspected he'd already had a little taste of Cam's bedtime snack.

"You're not feeding it to Sarge, are you?"

"A little bite won't hurt him. He loved it."

"Where has my husband gone?" she asked in dismay.

He shrugged and had the grace to look uncomfortable. "I'll do better tomorrow, but you know I can't get to sleep when I'm hungry."

"Oh, Cam, what are we going to do?"

There was nothing more to be said tonight, but somehow she had to convince him that high blood pressure wasn't something that went away on its own.

The last thing Elena did before leaving for the day was to check on the coma patient. She stared at the patient's serene face and wondered where her mind was. Did people in a deep coma dream? Did they have any awareness of their surroundings? Was this kind-faced woman fighting a battle in her mind, trying to surface to the real world?

Elena walked over to the bed and took her limp hand, wishing she could communicate with her in some way.

"Someone must be missing you," she said in a soft voice. "I bet you have lots of friends who are wondering where you are."

It didn't make sense that a well-dressed, middle-aged woman could disappear and no one noticed. Elena thought of different possibilities, but none made sense. People in Deerford didn't disappear without triggering an alarm.

She turned to leave when a new thought came to her. Maybe the patient didn't live in Deerford. She could have been passing through and stopped to stretch her legs, but where was her car? Someone would have reported an abandoned car by now. Anyway, the single key in her pocket appeared to be a house key and there was no driver's license.

When she got home, she planned to ask Cesar whether the police had any leads at all. She was afraid a person with a missing identity wasn't a priority with the department. The weather was warming faster than usual, and that meant more work for law enforcement. Criminals and rowdy people were always more active when spring arrived.

Elena left her coma patient somewhat reluctantly. She was getting good care around the clock, but Elena had this little nagging feeling that she could do something to help her. She couldn't place her face, but there was something familiar about it.

She hoped to have a heart-to-heart talk with Cesar about going to the new class at church with her, but she wasn't sure what to say. She could talk to him about enriching their marriage and their lives by learning more about the Lord's call to service, but she was afraid his mind was still closed to the Word.

Sighing deeply, Elena wondered whether Cesar was right about her crowded schedule. She did take on a lot, but there was a good reason for everything she did. Maria was thrilled to hear about the progress on her granddaughter's quinceañera dress, even though it was far from finished. And there was no way she could beg off the task force as long as there was the threat of an epidemic.

As she walked into the house, Elena was thinking of ways to broach the subject without starting an argument with Cesar. She slipped out of her coat, but before she could hang it up, Izzy rushed up to her, her face flushed with pleasure.

"I'm going to a rehearsal," she said a bit breathlessly.

Rafael was home ahead of her, since it had been his turn to pick up Izzy. "Hi, Mama," Rafael said, coming up behind his daughter. "Izzy has to practice for her recital. She's really excited about her ballet lessons."

"Mama is going to watch me too." Izzy was making a production out of shrugging into her winter coat, until her father stepped up to help her.

"Sarah is going to meet us there. It's not her regular time with Izzy, but I thought she could be there to see how our little princess is doing."

"That's nice," Elena said, sincerely proud of the way her son was handling the situation with Izzy's mother.

He was calm and cooperative about letting Izzy spend time with Sarah. It was best for Izzy and for both of her parents.

"Oh, did you two have dinner?" she asked as they made their way to the door.

"Don't worry, Mama," Rafael said. "We had sandwiches and chips."

"Sandwiches and chips," Elena repeated, not impressed with her son's idea of dinner but glad he'd fed Izzy before she went to the extra dance session.

She went to the kitchen and pondered what she should fix for Cesar. Before she could decide, he came in through the back door, stomping his feet on the doormat because it had started to rain.

"You're home. It must be my lucky day," he said in a disgruntled voice, as he came into the kitchen, his hair still wet from the shower.

"That isn't fair. I'm almost always here to fix your supper."

"I suppose."

"Did you have a bad day? You sound as cheerful as a grizzly bear."

"Just the usual," Cesar said, draping his coat over the back of a kitchen chair. "What's for supper?"

"I haven't decided. What would you like?"

"It doesn't matter."

Elena gave him a puzzled look. Cesar always had definite ideas on what he wanted to eat.

"Then I'll take a pizza out of the freezer."

"Whatever."

"You know I don't like that word! What is the matter with you?"

"It just irks me that I practically have to make an appointment to spend time with my wife. If you're not out saving the world, you're hunched over your sewing machine making a fancy dress for someone you've never even met."

"It's only to help a patient. People recover better if they're not stressed."

"Is that in your nursing handbook?"

"It's common sense!"

Much to her surprise, he started laughing, a deep growly burst of humor.

"Why are you laughing?"

"Because you're priceless. You care so much that I can't help but adore you."

"Really?"

"Really!" He swept her into his arms for a big hug. "We don't have to have frozen pizza for dinner. Where are Rafael and Izzy?"

"At a dance rehearsal."

"We're alone then. I think I should take my best girl out for supper. Nothing fancy. We'll go to your mother's restaurant. We haven't eaten there in a while."

Elena smiled her approval.

"But before we go, you should know that I've been thinking about what we talked about earlier."

"Oh?"

"The new class at church."

"If you really object..."

"No, I know how much it means to you. Maybe I could go to the first class with you. I won't promise to go every time, but I'll give it a try, just so I can spend more time with my wife."

"Thank you, thank you." Her eyes got teary, knowing how much of a concession this was from her husband.

"Get your coat. We'll see what your mama has on special this evening."

Her smile came from her heart. She was indeed blessed to be married to a man like Cesar.

"Oh, one more thing," he said. "I've checked missing person reports for the whole county, and there's no one who remotely resembles your coma patient."

"That's so strange. I would swear she's not a homeless person. Someone should be missing her."

"If she lives on her own, her friends may be used to having her come and go whenever she likes. Eventually someone may notice newspapers piling up or an overflowing mailbox."

"I hope so. It's just not right for her to lie there with no one to care."

"You care, sweetheart. That's one of the reasons why I love you."

He pulled her into his arms and reminded her that, come what may, they had each other.

Chapter Eleven

CANDACE ENJOYED HAVING THURSDAY OFF, EVEN though it had meant working last Saturday. This week, she had time for a morning dental appointment, a trip to the bank, and a chance to shop for Brooke's birthday gift. She also met an old friend for lunch and had her hair done in the afternoon.

"You're in a happy mood," her mother said when she got home.

"I got a lot done and had a nice lunch, but I'm especially pleased by the outfits I found on sale for Brooke's birthday. She really needs spring and summer clothes."

Janet followed as she spread her purchases on the back of the couch for her inspection.

"What do you think? Will Brooke like them?"

"Oh dear, I don't know what she'll like anymore. I'm afraid I took the easy way and bought a gift card. The pink shirt is really sweet, but I don't know whether she'll like the balloon print on the yellow top. Some days she acts like a ten-year-old, and other times she could be going on twenty."

"I know what you mean," Candace said with a faint smile. "Well, we can return anything she doesn't like. It's fun to buy clothes for her, but she has a right to wear things she likes—within reason."

She returned the outfits to the plastic shopping bags and took them to her bedroom to gift wrap, hoping her daughter wouldn't think the paper she had on hand was too *babyish*, her favorite word lately.

On impulse she decided to treat herself to a real luxury, an afternoon nap. She just had time to sleep for an hour or so before picking up the children at school, a job she enjoyed since her mother usually did it.

When the alarm woke her, she felt refreshed and eager to see her children. Howie's school dismissed nearly half an hour before Brooke's, so she had time to chat with him and take him home before picking up her daughter.

"How was your day?" she asked him as he fastened his seat belt in the backseat.

"Tim was bad. He wrote on the chalkboard when the teacher wasn't looking."

The adventures of Tim, the class cutup, were a favorite topic with Howie. Although Howie seldom misbehaved, he was fascinated by the antics of his naughty classmate.

"Did he get in trouble?" Candace asked.

"No, he erased it before the teacher saw." Howie sounded a bit put out that the crime went undetected.

"What did you do today?"

"I fell down at recess; but I didn't bleed, so I didn't have to see the nurse. Can I watch *Captain 'Magination*?" he asked, and Candace stifled a laugh at his quick change of subject. The boy was so easily distracted.

"Do you mean *Captain Imagination*? Does Grammy let you watch him?"

"Sometimes," he said evasively.

"It's a cartoon, right?"

"Yeah. But Captain 'Magination helps people learn about stuff like flying to the moon."

"We'll see what Grammy says."

Candace was careful not to contradict any rules her mother established. It wasn't fair to her or the kids to send mixed signals.

"She'll ask if I have homework," Howie told her glumly.

"Do you?"

"Just a tiny, tiny, tiny bit. I can do it in a minute."

"Maybe, but can you do it well if you work that fast?"

"I guess not."

She went in the house with Howie long enough to check with her mother on cartoon viewing. Janet was strict about limiting how much Howie could watch. He was delighted when his grandmother agreed that *Captain Imagination* was a cut above most cartoons and had some educational value. Candace went off to get her daughter, leaving a happy little boy at home.

When she got to Brooke's middle school, the children were just spilling out of the building. She spotted her walking with several other girls, all of them so engrossed in their conversation that the group nearly walked past her car. Knowing how Brooke would hate it if she honked to get her attention, Candace slid out of the car and called her name just loud enough to get her attention.

At first Brooke didn't seem to hear her, so Candace called her name again somewhat louder. She turned her head this time and said something to the girl next to her. Candace was behind the steering wheel and buckled in before her daughter ran back and got into the car beside her.

"How could you yell at me like that in front of my friends?"

"You walked right past me. I didn't think you saw me." Candace tried not to show her frustration, but so many conversations with Brooke seemed to start off badly these days.

"Mother! How could I not see a car right in front of me? I was just walking Tiffany to her father's van."

Candace bit back a sarcastic comment about not being a mind reader and let a moment pass in silence while she pulled away from the curb.

"Tiffany is definitely having boys at her birthday party," Brooke said in a more conciliatory tone.

"That's her parents' decision."

"Next you'll tell me I can't even go to her party!"

"We'll talk about that another time."

"Mother, her birthday is in May. It's only two months away."

"Brooke, I need to concentrate on driving. You know how children dart out between parked cars by your school."

"They're *not* children," Brooke corrected her. "That's your problem, Mother. You don't realize that I'm practically grown.

There's no reason at all why I can't have boys at my birthday party. My friends won't even want to come if I don't."

"I'm sure they will. You're going to have a nice party."

Brooke was silent for several minutes, but Candace knew she wasn't going to give up. She was sulking, trying to think up more arguments in favor of a coed party.

Candace's objection was one her daughter would never accept: She was rushing into adulthood, wanting to be eighteen instead of thirteen. What would her father have done? Candace was sure Dean wouldn't have approved of dating at Brooke's age, and wasn't that the next step after a boy-girl party?

Brooke was silent until they pulled into the driveway and then she tried again.

"If you let me have boys at my party, I promise I won't fight with Howie for two months—no, six months."

Candace smiled to herself at her daughter's attempt at bargaining, but as the mother, she had to take it seriously. Brooke couldn't be allowed to get her way by making a promise she couldn't keep.

"They're two separate issues. One has nothing to do with the other," she said as gently as possible, turning off the engine but making no move to go inside.

"You're just doing this to punish me."

"Sweetheart, I have no reason to punish you."

"Then why can't I have a party with boys?"

"It doesn't seem like a good idea this year."

"That's not a reason to ruin my party."

Before Candace could say more, Brooke jumped out of the car without closing the door and hurried into the house.

What else could she have said? Candace was at her wit's end, feeling almost as if her daughter were a stranger. Did all parents of teens go through this period of alienation? How could she be the parent and make the hard decisions without losing something precious between her daughter and herself?

She sighed, got out of the car, and closed the door Brooke had left open.

Chapter Twelve

THE SEVEN MEMBERS OF JAMES'S TASK FORCE committee met at noon, bringing sack lunches. Maxine Newman met with them for this important meeting to plan the hospital's response to a major epidemic. They all agreed that a drill was essential so that everyone would be prepared for the worst.

The county health nurse apologized for scheduling it during their lunch break and brought homemade brownies for them to enjoy while they worked, but she let James take the lead.

"I made a chart of the goals we discussed previously," James said, holding up a sheet of poster board with neatly lettered points. "In any disaster, not only an epidemic, we have to be ready for a mass influx of patients because Hope Haven is a level II trauma center. Fortunately, we have Dr. Weller helping us. He was involved in a full-scale disaster drill during his internship."

He turned the meeting over to the Emergency Room doctor, who wasted no time getting down to business. The tall, slender doctor ran his hand through his somewhat unruly dark brown hair and launched into plans for the simulated epidemic.

"Local law enforcement and several service organizations are already on board. The trick is to use real people as mock patients without letting things get chaotic. We need good press so the public understands what's going on and why."

"Hopefully what we learn from this drill will carry over into other kinds of disasters," James added.

"We'll have extra staff and ambulances on hand," Dr. Weller said. "Mercy Hospital in Granville is going to cooperate one hundred percent."

James listened carefully, added his ideas, and took careful notes. His job would be to coordinate all the units inside the hospital. It was a heavy responsibility, and he prayed that he was up to it. If an epidemic did hit Deerford, the plans they were making now could mean the difference between life and death for some victims.

After the meeting, the rest of his day seemed quietly routine. The closest thing to a crisis was a patient who accused an LPN of stealing his wristwatch. James found it under his pillow and soothed the hurt feelings of the staff member.

After work he had one more meeting. He didn't have much hope that the pet detective would find Sapphire, but he was curious to see how she worked. His boys and the Scouts had papered the town with posters, even offering a reward to the finder. What more could be done to locate one lost cat?

He didn't want to get Fern's hopes up for nothing, so he'd asked the pet detective to meet him in the hospital cafeteria. There weren't many people there at this time of day, but he was told to look for a woman in a purple jacket. He spotted her immediately at a table on the far right, but she wasn't at all what he'd expected.

"Mimi Zonn," she said, standing when he walked up to the table.

She shook his hand with a firm grip and looked him directly in the eyes, not difficult since she was as tall or taller than his five eleven.

"Mr. Bell, I understand your kitty has gone AWOL." She settled her statuesque form on a chair that seemed too small for her larger-than-life presence and pulled out a sheaf of papers from a large briefcase. "I have your case history here and the copy of the flier that you faxed to our office."

"Then I guess you know about all there is to know about Sapphire," he said, wondering where this was going.

"Not quite. Does she have a history of wandering off?"

"Definitely not."

"You recently moved to a new neighborhood?"

"Yes, but she'd had some time to get used to the new yard," he answered.

"She was your wife's companion?"

"Yes, my wife has MS. She doesn't get out much during the day, so it would mean a lot to her to have Sapphire back. If that's possible, that is."

"Our agency has a ninety-two percent recovery rate," Mimi said, her large face beaming optimism.

She brushed aside a heavy swatch of dark brown hair that didn't quite go with her pale blue eyes and took out a glittery ballpoint pen to make notes.

"Are there other cats in your neighborhood, especially any that regularly roam around?"

"Not that I've noticed."

"Any dogs that have harassed her?"

"No."

"Is she a mouser? Does she like to chase birds?"

"No to both."

"Does she bring home little presents, say a shrew or a snake?"

"No, fortunately. She's pretty much an indoor pet. Where is all this going?"

"Just getting some background on your cat's personality."

James felt as if he'd tumbled into a grade-B detective movie. "I called you as a last resort."

"Yes, people always do. Would you say that your Sapphire would come home if nothing prevented her from doing so?"

"Yes, definitely," he said.

"So you would characterize her as a happy house pet?" she said, continuing her line of questioning.

"Of course."

"Then what we need is a plan of action. You need to form a search committee."

"My sons and the Boy Scouts have already looked all over town. I don't know what more I can do."

"You can knock on doors," she said decisively.

"I thought you—"

"Yes, clients always expect me to do all the footwork, but it doesn't work that way. What our agency does is lay out a plan. If you suspect that your cat is being held hostage, then we step in and do the dangerous part; but the preliminary work is up to you. You wouldn't want to pay our fees if we canvassed the neighborhood for you."

"I suppose not."

"Here's what you do," she said leaning across the table and speaking in a husky whisper.

"What will that accomplish?" he asked, more mystified than reluctant after she finished outlining her plan.

"Sapphire hasn't been left at animal control, and there's no evidence that she's been hit by a car. We have to assume that someone found her and took her home."

"She has an identity collar. Wouldn't the finder try to contact us?"

"Not if they want to keep her, but let's assume her collar was missing for some reason. There are people who will take in any number of strays. Your cat could be the prisoner of a cat lover."

James shook his head. This was not at all what he expected.

"I picked up a map of Deerford on my way here," Mimi said, spreading it out on the table and taking out a mechanical pencil. "If I have it right, your house is right here."

"Approximately," he said.

"We'll divide the immediate neighborhood into grids. I'm talking house-to-house canvassing here. Work in teams, especially the boys if you decide to enlist them. One asks the questions. The other tries to get a look inside. If there's any reason to believe there are multiple cats inside, use some excuse to get a better look. Ask for a drink of water or something."

"I can't see myself going to neighbors' houses and asking for water."

"I didn't say this would be easy, but I have a hunch about this case. We're not talking about a common alley cat here." Mimi lowered her voice even more. "The better the breed, the more likely it is that someone decided to adopt her."

What she said made sense, even though it wasn't what he'd expected from a pet detective.

"I'll give it a try, but hitting every house in the neighborhood is going to take more time than I have."

"Do your best," she said. "Now about my fee. I'm only charging you for two hours plus mileage for the trip from Peoria because I have another client to see just outside of Deerford."

She handed him a bill that made him blink with surprise, but he was willing to do whatever it took if Fern could get her companion back. Sapphire had picked an inopportune time to disappear, though. Until their old house was sold, money was tight.

"We take cash, check, or credit card," Mimi said, obviously expecting immediate payment.

James took out his billfold, not at all sure the advice he'd received was worth the price. He handed over his credit card with misgivings, but he supposed her advice was sound. The Scouts hadn't knocked on doors or poked their noses into people's houses. He couldn't imagine doing it himself, but if there was a chance of finding Sapphire, he supposed it was worth a try.

"Now Mr. Bell, call me if you don't get any results in the next week or so. The trail is already cold, but we may have a few more tricks up our sleeves." She lowered her voice to a whisper again. "In Peoria we busted a ring of pet shop owners shipping so-called lost pets down to Texas. I tell you, it wasn't pretty."

She left him without saying more, walking away in high-heeled boots and stiff navy jeans that made her legs look like tree trunks. Mimi Zonn was an imposing figure, but was she for real? Would her plan be any help at all in finding Sapphire?

James left for home, deciding not to say anything to Fern about the pet detective right now. His hopes weren't high, and he didn't want her to suffer another disappointment if the house-to-house grid plan didn't bring results.

When he got home, Fern met him at the door with a broad smile on her face. His first thought was that Sapphire had returned home and he'd paid the pet detective for nothing.

"Guess what?" she said.

"I'm fresh out of guesses. Maybe you can just tell me."

"The Realtor called. We've had an offer on our house, a good one. And the buyer is almost a shoo-in to get approved for a mortgage. Isn't it wonderful?" She looked happier than he'd seen her since her pet disappeared. He decided not to burst her bubble of happiness by telling her about the expensive advice from the pet detective.

The pleasure he should have been feeling over the sale of the house was tempered by his reluctance to follow Mimi Zonn's advice. How could he traipse all over town asking people if they'd stolen his cat?

Chapter Thirteen

Elena's house was quiet except for the soft purring of her sewing machine. Thankfully, everyone in the family slept soundly, especially Cesar. She loved working on the luxurious fabric of the quinceañera dress, and she felt privileged to be able to finish it. Satisfied that there was nothing more she could do on the machine, she carefully gathered up the gown and worked it onto the dress dummy she'd borrowed and adjusted to fit the young girl's form.

"Perfect," she said to herself.

Now all she had to do was hem it. She'd considered using an iron-on seam tape, but she opted instead for fine, hand-sewn stitching. It would take longer, but a dress this beautiful and important deserved the best finishing details.

She glanced at her wristwatch and was surprised to see how late it was. When she was involved in a sewing project, time flew. Cesar might be cross with her for staying up so late, but it was a labor of love.

Intending to do just a little more, she hemmed until her eyelids were drooping shut. When she finally gave up, there was only a few hours of work left. It could easily be completed the next day.

Her alarm rang far too soon Friday morning, but she was still excited by how nicely the dress was turning out. She left for work a bit reluctantly because it really would have been nice to finish the hem.

"James, I have a new word for you," Elena said as she caught up with him in the parking lot on her way into the hospital.

"Oh I'd love to chat, Elena, but I just don't have much time. Later?" he said, walking toward the entrance at such a fast pace that she nearly had to run to catch up.

"Later is fine," she said, surprised that he didn't want to play their favorite game. "I'm pretty sure I have a word that will stump you."

"I'm stumped by more than words," he said in a glum voice that was totally unlike his usual good-natured banter.

"Did Fern have a setback?" she asked.

"No, nothing like that. Fern is doing well. The boys are fine."

"Well, I understand that you have a lot on your mind with the task force and the preparedness drill," she said sympathetically. "You have so much responsibility."

"Elena, if you want to know why I'm a bear this morning, just ask."

She was stunned. James was the most even-tempered person she knew, so he must be particularly irritated to snap at her like that.

"You do seem out of sorts," she said as mildly as possible. "Is there something I can do to help?"

"Not unless you want to knock on doors and peep into houses."

"Something to do with Sapphire?" she asked cautiously.

"Everything to do with her. I hired a pet detective, but it turns out that she only gives advice. She thinks I should check every house in town to see if someone has Sapphire. She even divided Deerford into grids."

"Every house in town! Even in a small town like ours, that could take forever."

"That's if people stay home to answer doors. I covered two blocks last night, and thirteen owners weren't home. Those who answered either thought I was loony, or they were insulted that I thought they had our cat. My boys tried another block and didn't have any better luck. Worse, I had to tell Fern what we were doing. I didn't want to get her hopes up, but what excuse could I give for the three of us being out late?"

"It doesn't sound like the pet detective was much help."

"If I uncover a ring of stolen pets, she'll spring into action and bring them down," he said. "Meanwhile, I don't know whether to give up and buy Fern a new cat or keep knocking."

"Maybe Cesar and I could help—"

"Thank you for offering, but I wouldn't think of dragging either of you into it."

He held the door for her but didn't go to the elevator. Whatever he had to do on the main floor, he wasn't in the mood to talk to her anymore. She watched him walk away, sorry that the missing cat was causing so much distress. She couldn't remember ever seeing James so cross.

In the staff lounge she found Anabelle combing her hair before beginning work for the day.

"Good morning," Elena said, expecting a cheerful reply.

"Not so far," Anabelle said in an unhappy voice.

"Oh dear, not you too. Today was the first time I've seen James truly out of sorts, all because of a lost cat."

"I thought he was going to hire a pet detective."

"He did. That's the problem. It seems pet detectives don't actually find pets. They just tell the client how to proceed. James is supposed to canvass every house in town to see if anyone took in Sapphire."

"That's not possible, not for someone as busy as James."

"His sons are helping, but it's still terribly frustrating."

"I know how he feels. I seem to have lost my husband."

"What?" Elena asked with alarm.

"I'm exaggerating," Anabelle quickly explained. "But he certainly hasn't been himself since his high blood pressure was diagnosed. One good thing, though. He signed up for an exercise class at the YMCA. He's going for the first time this morning, but not with a very good attitude. You'd think he was going off to marine boot camp the way he complained."

"I thought he was pretty fit."

"He is, and the class is geared to retired men. He'll probably enjoy it once he gets started. He just doesn't like the idea of changing his lifestyle, especially what he eats."

"Well, good luck on that. I'm off to work," Elena said.

In midmorning, Dr. Hamilton visited the ICU to check on the coma patient. Elena always welcomed his visits because he was unfailingly courteous and good-natured, unlike a few doctors who barked orders and expected the nurses to do their bidding instantly.

"We have a dilemma," Dr. Hamilton said after spending some time with the patient. "I can't believe no one has reported her missing. There are decisions to be made. We need to move her to a long-term care facility, but without knowing her insurance status, our hands are tied. I hesitate to have her declared a ward of the state if she has relatives."

"There's something vaguely familiar about her," Elena mused. "I wish I knew what."

"Speculation is no help," the doctor snapped. "We need to know who this woman is."

"Yes sir," Elena meekly agreed, wondering what had gotten into the men of Deerford on this sunny March day.

First James had been unusually cross and then Cameron was unhappy about an exercise class. Now her favorite doctor was cranky. If the men in her family had the crabby-bug too, she'd be better off working a double shift.

The morning went by slowly, filled with lots of routine and not much patient progress. At least they weren't in crisis mode, and the waiting room wasn't full of anxious relatives who needed reassurance. By the time her lunch break came, Elena was hungry and weary.

She was grateful the cafeteria line was thankfully short, and she loaded her tray with salad, macaroni and cheese, and bread pudding, adding a cloverleaf roll for good measure. It was double the lunch she usually ate, but she felt in need of fuel to get through the rest of her shift. She didn't see any of her close friends, so she took a small table by the far wall.

She wasn't usually a food critic, but the macaroni seemed a little tough, and the roll had to be day-old. At least the salad greens were fresh and crisp. She was about to taste test the bread pudding when Sarah came up to her table wearing a large chef's apron that made her look even more frail and a hairnet over her pale hair, standard dress for the kitchen workers.

"Do you mind if I join you for a minute?" she asked.

"Love to have you," Elena said, motioning for Izzy's mother to sit.

"I saw you go through the line. The head cook said I could take a short break."

"How is your job going?" Elena asked conversationally.

"Oh, I like the kitchen workers. They work hard, but they're almost always cheerful. Is there something wrong with the macaroni? I could take it back for you and get something else."

"No, I just overestimated my appetite," Elena said, not wanting to make a fuss about it.

"There's something I wanted to ask you."

Elena took a deep breath, hoping her question had nothing to do with Rafael or Izzy. As far as she knew, they'd come to an arrangement that both parents could live with. Izzy was happy to have her mother in her life, but it didn't in any way diminish her love for her father or grandparents. Nor did it affect her granddaughter's living with them. Rafael still had full custody, but he was wisely letting Izzy get to know her mother.

"All right," Elena said cautiously.

"Have you noticed that a new cookware store has opened up downtown where the bookstore used to be?"

"I may have read something about it in the newspaper, but I haven't actually seen it."

"It's quite nice. I never imagined how many different things are available for the kitchen. The owner is starting some cooking classes. The back of the store is set up as a kitchen. I picked up this list of the classes."

She handed a sheet of yellow paper to Elena and gave her a minute to read it.

"My, she's offering quite a variety. I have a friend who may be interested in the healthy cooking class. Do you mind if I keep this?"

"Please do. I pretty much have it memorized."

"What did you want to ask me?"

"I like working in the kitchen, but I haven't decided whether to make a career in food preparation. Meanwhile, I wonder whether I should take a beginning cooking class. It might help me move into an assistant cook's job here and give me a better idea of whether it's right for me. Of course, it might be a waste of time and money if I decide to do something else."

"It's never a waste of time to learn something new," Elena said. "The important thing is whether it's something you would enjoy and find worthwhile. Only you can decide that."

"I can always rely on you to say something sensible," Sarah said with a small smile. "Maybe I'll put it off for now and give it some more thought. How was Isabel this morning?"

"I left for work too early to see her. But I did lay out her clothes for the day. She's wearing navy-blue leggings with a sunny yellow hoodie jacket over a white long-sleeved T-shirt. The yellow is a nice contrast to her dark hair. No doubt she'll look darling. But then, she always does."

"Thank you," Sarah said. "It makes the work go faster if I have an image of Isabel in my mind. Well, I'd better get back to the kitchen."

"I'm glad you came out to join me," Elena said. "And I'm really happy to learn about the cooking classes. I may know someone who will be interested."

Elena didn't have a chance to speak to Anabelle until their shift was over for the day, but she managed to catch up with her in the parking lot.

"I have an idea for you," she called over to her friend.

Anabelle turned and waited for her, a puzzled expression on her patrician features.

"Actually, Izzy's mother gave me the idea. There's a new cookware shop downtown, where Francie's Books and Things used to be. I haven't been there, but Sarah said they have quite a stock of kitchen utensils and such."

"I think I heard something about it, but our kitchen is pretty well stocked already."

"Oh, I'm not suggesting you buy new pots or anything, but the owner is giving cooking lessons. The back of the store is a big kitchen, and some of her classes sound interesting. I especially noticed one on healthy cooking. If Cameron is taking an interest in the culinary arts, this might be something to check out."

"You might be right," Anabelle said thoughtfully. "I don't know whether he would try cooking lessons, but he does have free time to occupy. Maybe I'll sound him out and see what he says. Thanks for telling me."

"My pleasure," Elena said, glad that she'd passed on the information Sarah had given her. "Here, you can take this class list home with you."

Her happy mood lasted until she got home and spotted trouble. Rafael's van was in the middle of the driveway with the hood up, a pair of jean-clad legs sticking out. She didn't need to see her son's face to know that he was working on the motor.

She parked her car on the street and walked over to him.

"What's wrong?"

"Mama, if I knew what was wrong, I wouldn't be standing on my head trying to figure it out."

"Did you pick up Izzy?"

"No, I had to call Daddy to pick her up. The motor died so many times I barely made it home from the restaurant." He straightened with a sour expression on his face. "Not only that, I have a class tonight, and the band has an important gig this Saturday. How will we transport our instruments if this old heap won't run?"

"Tonight is no problem. You can use my car. And Izzy is probably having the time of her life at the police station. I wonder if they really give ice cream cones to stray kids."

"Sounds like something that happens in comic strips," her son said sounding unusually peeved. "I don't know whether to have this wreck towed to a garage or a junkyard."

"Maybe it's not as serious as you think. Wait until your father gets home. He'll know what to do."

"Mama, you know as much about cars as I know about nursing."

It was true, but she didn't like the way he said it. "Don't be sassy to your mother."

"Sorry, but this is a really bad time for the van to break down." He slammed the hood down and went to the house to call a friend who knew more about motors than he did.

Elena followed, wondering whether Rafael was upset about more than the van. He had a lot on his plate, including the big decision he'd made to be a policeman. It could be a long, slow process to get hired. He couldn't be admitted to the police academy until he actually had a job lined up, and patience wasn't his strongest characteristic. Maybe he was overreacting to vehicle trouble because he was frustrated by the length of time it would take to actually become a cop.

Anyway, she'd had enough of crabby men. She still couldn't believe that James, Cameron, and Dr. Hamilton were out of sorts on the same day, not to mention Rafael. If Cesar wasn't in a better mood than his son, it would end up as a perfectly awful day. Rafael's friend came, and he went back to the van. When she glanced out, they both had their heads buried in the inner workings of the vehicle.

After changing clothes and starting dinner, Elena sat down in her bedroom to complete a few last-minute touches to the quinceañera dress. She'd just finished it and returned to the kitchen as Cesar came through the carport door with Izzy riding on his shoulders.

"Look what I found!" he teased, prancing around as she laughed uproariously.

"I'm too big for pony rides," Izzy sputtered, her happy giggles making Elena smile.

Cesar lowered her to the floor, and she immediately began telling Elena about the police station.

"I'm going to be a policeman and put bad people in jail when I grow up," she announced.

"Oh, *mi bonita*," Cesar said, affectionately calling her "my pretty one" in Spanish, "you can't do that."

Izzy's face fell, but her grandfather quickly brought her smile back.

"You will have to be a policewoman. That's an even better thing to be."

"Now go change your clothes and wash up for dinner," Elena told her.

"Something smells good," Cesar said, giving his wife a big hug when their granddaughter left the room. "I think maybe it's you."

"Silly, it's the onion and cilantro in the salsa."

"How can a wife as sweet as mine not have the fragrance of flowers?" he teased.

"What's gotten into you?" she asked laughing.

"Do I have to wait for a special occasion to tell my wife how much I love her?"

"Please don't," she said turning to him with a warm smile. "I believe you're the best-natured man in town today."

She asked Rafael's friend to join them for supper, grateful that he'd found the trouble with the van and fixed it. They had just sat down at the table when the doorbell rang.

"Are you expecting someone?" Cesar asked.

"I'd forgotten. Maria Acuna's husband is picking up the quinceañera dress. She's scheduled to be dismissed from the hospital tomorrow, and he thought it would make her very happy to see the completed gown when she gets home."

Elena got up from the table, but she didn't miss the disgruntled look on her husband's face.

"I thought you still had a lot to do on it."

"Oh, it went faster than I thought." She hurried to the door before Cesar could ask more about how she'd finished it so quickly. The truth was, she'd worked into the small hours of the night. She didn't like deceiving her soundly sleeping husband, but it would only make him unhappy if he knew how she had pushed herself to finish.

"Mr. Acuna, won't you come in?" she asked the short, gray-haired man who stood outside her door.

"Oh, no thank you. I don't want to trouble you."

"Just give me a minute to get the dress," she said, dashing to her bedroom where she'd hung it in the closet.

It was a lovely creation, shimmering white with dainty lace on the bodice. Elena had truly loved working on it, daydreaming about the day when she might make a wedding dress for Izzy.

When she handed it over to Maria's husband, his face glowed with pleasure.

"Can I pay you for your trouble?" he asked in a soft voice.

"Oh no, I won't hear of it. I loved finishing it. It's the most beautiful gown I've ever sewn."

He thanked her profusely, and she was just closing the door when Cesar came to the entryway to see what was keeping her.

She sighed at her husband, sad to see the dress go. "I learned a lot from sewing that dress, and who knows? Maybe someday I'll make Izzy's wedding dress."

Cesar sighed at her, but she read the pride in his eyes.

"Rafael wants to drop a bombshell on you, but he's feeling guilty about it," he said. "I want you to know that you can say no, even if it's for Izzy."

"What are you talking about?"

"I guess I'd better warn you. Izzy needs a costume for her ballet recital, something fancy and frilly."

"You know I can't say no to that," she said. "Anyway, how much time will it take to make a dance costume?"

Cesar shook his head and smiled at her.

"Promise me you won't sneak out of bed again when you think I'm asleep," he said with mock sternness.

She gave him a quick hug and hurried back to the dinner table.

Chapter Fourteen

"I THOUGHT I MIGHT SEE IF EVAN NEEDS ANY HELP today," Cameron said to Anabelle after they finished a breakfast of bran cereal, fruit, and yogurt on Saturday morning.

Anabelle gave him a wifely look across the table. "You promised we could check out the new cookware store this morning."

"I didn't exactly promise," he hedged. "I only said maybe."

His wife shook her head. "You never used the word *maybe*."

"Working in the business is good for me. It gets me outside. I'd much rather do some landscaping than take that class at the Y. Last time the instructor had us stepping on and off risers. Where's the sense in that?"

"It was probably part of a full-body workout," she suggested. "Anyway, it's only March 12. I can't believe the ground is soft enough to start planting."

"We're having an early spring."

"Not that early. It might be nice this week, but we could still get some late snow. I'm sure Evan hasn't started any projects that require your help."

"I can't believe that you expect me to take cooking lessons," he said, carrying his dishes to the sink. "You don't want me to eat anything I like, so why go to a class?"

"You don't have to sign up today. Let's just visit the store and see what the setup is. Maybe after you meet the owner who's teaching the classes, you'll feel differently."

"Who takes cooking classes anyway? New brides who can't boil water? Women who don't know what to do with their time? I don't want to be the only rooster at a hen party."

"I can't believe you said that!" Anabelle said, beginning to believe that her dear, sweet husband had been switched with a look-alike.

"If it will make you happy, I'll go with you to check it out," he said, giving her the sweet little grin that confirmed he was indeed her husband.

"Thank you," she said. "That's all I ask."

Once he'd committed himself, Cam was a good sport about driving into town and parking near the Chef's Corner. Anabelle wasn't sure what to expect, but as soon as she stepped through the door, she was impressed by the way the old store had been renovated. They slowly wandered among shelves of shiny new appliances and cookware, and even Cameron was impressed by the variety of goods on sale.

"Goodness," Anabelle said. "Our kitchen is certainly outdated compared to all these new things. Look at this mixer!"

"Costs as much as a good used car," Cam said in a soft voice. "You're not thinking of buying a lot of new stuff, are you?"

"No, that's not why we're here."

Anabelle knew how old most of her equipment was, but she wouldn't trade it for high-tech gadgets. So many things in her kitchen had sentimental value. Her children had given her a waffle iron for Christmas when they were still in grade school, and her shelves were still full of wedding gifts that she used all the time. She fondly remembered her Aunt Betty every time she cooked in one of the set of copper-bottomed kettles. She had a wicked-looking knife that had been handed down from her grandmother. In fact, she'd always kept it on a high shelf away from her children, and now that she had a grandchild, it would stay there. Cam laughed at her whenever he saw her using it, which was seldom, but there was nothing like it to halve squash or slice watermelon.

"Is there something I can help you with?"

A soft-spoken voice with a southern accent brought her attention back to the present. She turned to see a pleasingly plump woman with a huge mane of teased yellow hair and lively blue eyes. She was wearing a pink-and-white-striped cotton dress and a fluffy apron that tied at the back. Anabelle couldn't remember seeing anyone in a fancy little apron for ages.

"We're just looking," Cam said.

"Actually," Anabelle said, "we came to find out more about your cooking classes."

"Just out of curiosity," her husband added, trying to make it clear that they weren't there to sign up.

"Splendid," she said enthusiastically. "I'm Sherry Randall. This is my store, and I'll be teaching most of the classes for now. I grew up just outside of Atlanta, so you might say there will be a southern flavor in many of the recipes we'll be cooking. But let me show you the kitchen first."

They followed her to the rear of the long store, and Anabelle was pleasantly surprised by the ultraefficient setup. There were several long, gleaming white counters; two sets of double ovens; and a restaurant-sized refrigerator. Pots and pans hung from ceiling hooks, and there seemed to be more than enough to accommodate a fairly large class. Countertop burners, a large double sink, and glass-fronted cupboards all had a new, sparkling clean look; and long rubber mats provided foot comfort for people working in the space.

"As you've probably guessed, I'm new in Deerford," Sherry said. "My husband was career air force until he retired, and we lived all over the world. I like to think I learned some new culinary tricks every place we went. We were living in Omaha when he passed away."

"That's a shame," Anabelle said. "Losing your husband, not living in Omaha. How did you pick Deerford to open a business?"

"I used to visit a dear friend here. Sadly, she's passed away too, but I always loved coming here. It's my idea of a picture-perfect small town, and the people I've met so far haven't disappointed me. Everyone has been so friendly and kind. And what do you folks do?"

"My wife is a nurse at Hope Haven Hospital," Cam said, answering before Anabelle could. "I recently turned my landscaping business over to our son, but I still like to keep my hand in. I'm Cameron Scott. This is Anabelle."

"I'm so pleased to meet you both. I never would've taken you for a retired man, Mr. Scott." She offered her hand, first to Anabelle, then to him.

"Just call me Cam."

"This is where we hold our classes," she said, gesturing at the impressive setup.

"Do you have other teachers?" Anabelle asked.

"Just one at the present. A young lady from the community college will be offering classes in pastry. I never did get the knack for making perfect Greek pastries like hers, but I'll be teaching the rest for now, just good old home cooking, southern style. What's your favorite Sunday dinner, Cam?"

"I'm partial to fried chicken."

"A man after my own heart. I dip my chicken in a secret recipe batter and deep-fry it and then serve it with zesty coleslaw and mashed sweet potatoes."

"Sounds great," Cam said.

"Of course, I love to finish with chocolate chip pecan pie. I still use a recipe passed down by my great granny."

"Sometimes they're the best ones," he said.

"Actually, we're interested in healthy cooking," Anabelle said with a sideways look at her husband. "Your flier mentioned it as one of the courses."

"Yes, I have some delicious vegetarian recipes," Sherry said. "Some you'd never miss the meat."

"I'm not exactly a vegetarian," Cam said, "but I'm willing to try new things."

Anabelle couldn't imagine getting him to eat stew without meat or tofu stir-fry, but at least he wasn't showing any hostility to the idea of different foods.

"About the courses..." she began.

"Here I am chattering away," Sherry said with a laugh. "Let me tell you how I operate. First, my list of course offerings."

She went to a drawer and took out a printed list.

"I have a sign-up sheet for each course. Whenever enough people register, I start a class. The minimum is five, and the maximum twelve students. Each will meet for three sessions; but if everyone is having a good time, we can extend it."

"So if a person signs up, there's no guarantee you'll be offering the course?" Anabelle asked.

"No, but I'm confident that people will bring their friends, and most classes will start without a long wait. Here's my fee schedule." She handed Cam another sheet of paper. "It varies a little depending on how expensive the ingredients are. Of course, after we cook, we eat. So come hungry and be ready for a taste treat."

Anabelle looked over Cam's shoulder at the fee sheet. It was a little more expensive than she'd expected, but certainly not too costly when her husband's health was at stake.

"The fee includes an apron you can keep," Sherry said. "There's nothing to bring, only your own sweet self, but I do ask that you wear closed-toe shoes for safety reasons."

"Good idea," Cam said. "The whole program sounds great to me."

Anabelle raised an eyebrow at his unexpected enthusiasm,

"Now, who's the chef in the family?" the buoyant blonde asked.

"Me," Cam said. "That is, I'm learning to be the family cook. Anabelle puts in long hours at the hospital, and I pretty much set my own work time."

"Splendid! You know, Cam, more and more men are getting into cooking. I think it's because of the chefs on television food programs. There's something so appealing about a man who can create a wonderful meal." She purred with enthusiasm.

"Well, should we sign up now?" Cam asked Anabelle.

"Should we sign up? I thought you—"

"A couple cooking together is so romantic," Sherry said. "My husband and I shared some wonderful moments over a stove, although he did prefer to grill outside. I can remember him shoveling snow to get to our gas grill. Food tasted even better when he went to so much trouble."

"The plan was—" Anabelle began again.

"I think we'll start with the Happy Heart course," Cam said decisively.

"You'll love that one," Sherry said. "I even include a simple little dessert with hardly any calories but loads of taste."

"Imagine that," Cam said. "I can't wait to get started."

He took the sign-up sheet she gave him and wrote both their names.

"Now, is there anything else I can do for you today?" the storeowner asked.

"There is one thing we could use," Cam said. "I'm about ready to throw our old can opener into the trash. What do you have that will rip open cans with no sweat?"

"Let me show you our best electric model."

Ten minutes later they left the store. Cam was carrying a sack with an opener that reminded Anabelle of a jet motor and a vegetable peeler that was so sharp it would probably require first aid when he used it.

"That wasn't so bad," he said.

"I didn't plan to take cooking lessons myself."

"It will be fun. Sherry said she's had several couples sign up for different courses."

"Cam, I'm so busy at the hospital. The task force is planning a drill in case we have an epidemic and—"

"You need some recreation. What could be nicer than doing something together?"

She didn't have an answer to that. Apparently, she was going to take cooking classes. She wasn't looking forward to them, but her mood brightened that afternoon when her daughter Ainslee dropped off Lindsay Belle so she could shop without taking her little daughter with her.

"I really appreciate this, Mother," Ainslee said. "Doug has some work he has to catch up on, and it's really hard taking Lindsay Belle from store to store when she's all bundled up."

Anabelle had to smile at her little granddaughter. She was encased in a pink snowsuit that made her look as wide as she was tall. She sat down on the floor to pull off Lindsay Belle's shiny white boots and unzip the suit.

"What have we here?" Cam asked, coming into the entryway.

"Hi, Pop. Thanks to both of you for babysitting," Ainslee said. "I'll be leaving now if you don't mind. Everything you might need is in the diaper bag, including a fresh outfit if Grandpa tries to teach her to eat an ice cream cone again."

"I think we'll pass on that," Anabelle said with a light laugh. "When our little sweetheart comes, I have to watch two babies."

"We just know how to have fun, don't we, sweetheart?" Cam said, picking her up before Anabelle could help her wiggle out of her hooded snowsuit.

He plopped her down on the couch and somewhat awkwardly managed to remove her snowsuit and then the two of them went to the dining room where they had a collection of toys in a special plastic box, some left from their own children and others new.

Anabelle grinned broadly as her husband took Lindsay Belle's hand and shortened his stride to match the baby's none too steady gait. She was dressed in bright yellow tights and a blue knit dress with orange and yellow kittens in the pattern. Who knew that a tiny little person could bring so much joy to both of them?

Her enjoyment was interrupted by a sobering thought. If Cam wanted to watch his granddaughter grow up, he was going to have to take better care of himself. Hopefully, the cooking class would contribute to his understanding of what healthy eating was.

"Nana," Lindsay Belle said, summoning her grandmother to join in the fun.

Anabelle followed the pair into the living room where they quickly spread the toys out on the carpet. What could possibly be more fun than entertaining their beloved granddaughter?

Elena was delighted when Rafael was able to get the van running for a fee that he could handle on his small salary at the restaurant. She scarcely listened when he explained the intricacies of the aging motor, but the bottom line was that the band would get to their Saturday night gig. She watched as he and his friend loaded his equipment before leaving to collect the other members of the band.

She thought they had gone, but Rafael rushed back into the house, waving a plastic bag.

"I almost forgot. I had the directions for Izzy's costume in the van. I hope it won't take too much time to make it."

"I wonder what parents do when they don't sew," Elena teased, taking the directions out of the bag.

"Oh, there's a lady who will make them, but she charges quite a bit. I really appreciate your help," Rafael said.

"That's okay. It's fun to sew for Izzy."

"I'll be late, but I have my house key," her son assured her.

As the door closed behind him, she shook out the directions for the costume along with a swatch of pink netting and another of pink satin. The pattern wasn't too complicated. Izzy was in the youngest group, but the teacher still expected all the children to have appropriate costumes.

Elena smiled a bit ruefully. Izzy's part in the program would probably last two minutes at the most, but making the costume would take at least two evenings. The hard part would be finding the netting and matching the fabric color. She hoped it wouldn't involve a trip to Peoria. She would have to shop as soon as possible so the local store wouldn't be sold out.

The important thing was that Izzy would be thrilled. Elena could visualize her in a pretty pink tutu, which reminded her that she would also need pink tights. She hoped that the ballet teacher had checked on availability before she decided what the children should wear. If worse came to worst, she could dye a pair of Izzy's white tights.

Cesar was in the living room fiddling with the TV remote. "I have an idea. Let's rent a movie to watch after Izzy goes to bed. Maybe make some popcorn and snuggle on the couch?"

"Sounds nice," Elena said, forcing a smile.

She'd hoped to take a long, hot bath and get to bed really early; but she didn't want Cesar to think she was too tired to spend time with him.

"Izzy can come with us and pick out something she would like to watch tomorrow."

"It's nearly her bedtime. Why don't you go while I get her ready for bed?"

"You might not like what I pick out."

"Just so long as it's not one of those violent police movies. I worry about your job enough."

"Movies are fantasy. I'd like to see how movie bad guys would do in a real court of law."

"No cop movies," Elena said emphatically. "And I'd rather you didn't get some science-fiction flick that doesn't make sense."

"See why you should come with me?"

"No, I'll put Izzy to bed. She'll be up early tomorrow for Sunday school."

"That's a plan," he said, "but don't blame me if you don't like what I pick."

Elena was pretty sure it didn't matter. She would probably be sound asleep on the couch before it was half over anyway.

Before she could start Izzy's bath, the phone rang. She answered it a bit reluctantly, hoping it wasn't an emergency at the hospital that would require overtime work.

"Elena, this is Maggie Owens from church. Have you heard about the big pie sale the women's group is holding to raise money for disaster relief?"

"Yes, I think I read about it in last week's bulletin."

"We're asking everyone to donate pies. It's such a good cause with all the earthquakes and floods. Can I put you down for three?"

"Three pies? When would you need them?"

"You can drop them off Saturday or before the service Sunday."

"That's next weekend?"

"Yes. They can be any flavor. We're a little short on fruit pies: cherry, apple, or any kind of berry."

"Cherry, I could do cherry," Elena said. She would use a canned pie filling, much quicker than peeling apples which weren't that great this time of year anyway.

"Great, thanks so much, Elena."

Had she just agreed to make three pies? She'd have to make homemade crust to make up for the canned filling. Some of the women would make luscious creations that were sure to be popular. It would be embarrassing if her pies were the only ones that didn't sell.

She put the costume directions on her sewing machine so she wouldn't have to hunt for them to take to work Monday morning. Did she have a task force meeting after work that day? She was too tired to remember, but one happy thought kept her going. Cesar was going to the pastor's new class with her tomorrow evening.

Dear Lord, please let this small beginning open Cesar's heart to faith, she prayed.

"Grandmother!" Izzy called in her most demanding tone. "I need you!"

Elena walked into her granddaughter's bedroom and gave her a weary smile.

"I forgot about the things. I have to take them to school on Monday."

"What things?" Elena searched her mind but couldn't remember a note from the teacher that mentioned bringing anything to school.

"You know, I have to bring three things that can be 'cycled."

"Do you mean recycled?"

"Yes, the note was in my backpack."

"But you didn't show it to me."

"I forgot, but I have to take them."

"Well, I'm glad you think it's important to do your homework, but I wish you'd shown me the note when you came home from school Friday."

Had she even been home right after school? Elena wondered whether she was being unfair to Izzy. Her granddaughter often bubbled over with excitement about things that happened in school, but once she'd given her news of the day to any adult in the family, she completely put it out of her mind.

"I told Daddy."

"Well, let's look in our bins in the garage and see what we have."

It should have been simple, but everything in their bins had been picked up Friday, leaving little for Izzy to take to school. There was a vinegar bottle, but Elena vetoed taking glass to school. The only tin can had a sharp edge, another no-no as far as Elena was concerned.

She found last week's church bulletin in a basket on the kitchen counter and finally convinced Izzy that it was large enough to recycle. Izzy turned down a section of newspaper but agreed to take a magazine of Elena's that was two months old but still unread because she simply hadn't had time.

They were still searching for a third item when Cesar got home with a movie about penguins.

"The clerk said it was really good," he said.

"Can I watch too?" Izzy asked.

"Maybe tomorrow," Cesar said. "Isn't it past your bedtime?"

Elena explained the difficulty they were having, and he saved the day by donating a plastic cup he'd gotten at a basketball game last year.

Cesar volunteered to read a story when Izzy was finally tucked into bed, which gave Elena time for a quick shower. She joined him in the living room and settled down on the couch with her head on his shoulder.

The only penguins she saw were in her dreams.

Chapter Fifteen

SUNDAYS WERE BITTERSWEET FOR CANDACE. SHE loved having the day off and taking her children to Sunday school. Howie had learned not to squirm and whisper so much during the church service, and Brooke was eager to attend because she often sat with a friend. Still, she couldn't help remembering how Dean had helped her carry baby equipment, dry cereal, and quiet games to keep their children happy during the service. The days when he read the Scripture lesson were her favorites, and she could still remember his melodious voice bringing life to Bible passages.

Before the service began, while Howie was whispering earnestly to his grandmother, she silently thanked the Lord for the many blessings in her life. For years her heart had been frozen and she couldn't imagine finding happiness with another man, yet now she was in love with Heath Carlson. Today she prayed for the wisdom she and Heath needed to determine the next steps in their relationship.

"Grammy said to ask you if I can go to her old friend's house after lunch," Howie asked urgently, interrupting Candace's silent prayer.

Candace looked over at her mother and saw her nod of approval. Some Sundays Janet liked to call on an elderly friend Agnes. Howie loved to go with her because she had a player piano and lots of rolls to go with it. Agnes let him pump away at it, even providing a low stool so his feet could reach the pedals.

"All right," Candace said, "if you're very good in church."

That afternoon she found herself home alone with Brooke for the first time in several days. She hadn't mentioned her birthday party lately, and Candace hoped that meant she'd given up on wanting boys to attend.

She was wrong.

As soon as Janet and Howie left the house for their visit, Brooke found Candace in the kitchen making a batch of cookies for the children's lunches that week.

"Mother, we need to talk," Brooke said.

"We can do that," Candace said with a smile she hoped would start her daughter off on the right foot. "What's up?"

"I know my birthday party is going to be awful. My friends want to do something besides stand around and talk to each other."

Candace had so little experience in dealing with this end-of-the-world mentality. She steadied her nerves, trying to keep her cool. "I think we have a lot planned, honey. We've discussed this. There are games, use of the Y's facilities—"

"*You* have a lot planned."

"That's not fair," Candace said, using one of her daughter's favorite phrases. "You wanted to have it at the Y. You chose the refreshments."

"Please, Mother, it's not about where we're having it. Tiffany is having boys at her party. I don't know why I can't."

"Oh, Brooke, we've already talked about this too many times." She knew it was futile to go over the same arguments again.

"You've talked about it. You never listen to my side."

Candace's first instinct was to deny her daughter's accusation, but it was like talking to a brick wall.

"I only want to invite nice boys," Brooke wailed, getting increasingly dramatic. "Not boys who get in trouble or anything like that."

"I don't know what more to say," Candace said in a weary voice. "I'm the mother. Sometimes mothers have to make decisions their children don't like or understand."

"Mother, there you go again with the 'children' stuff. You still think I'm a child. I'll be a teenager, Mother. Doesn't that mean anything to you?"

Candace was beginning to think it meant one long argument, but she didn't say so. And the most ironic part was that Brooke was acting more like a child than ever.

"Do you want me to cancel the party?" She wasn't sure that the Y would refund her deposit, but she was at her wit's end.

"No! Everyone has a party when they're thirteen. I just want mine to be a fun party."

"You have a lot of friends. I'm sure they'll enjoy getting together."

"Oh, Mother. You don't understand."

Candace thought that she understood only too well. She only shook her head in frustration.

"Will you do one thing for me, just one small thing?" Brooke asked. "Please, please, just think about it. Don't say no for sure. Is that too much to ask?"

"All right. I'll think about it, but don't get your hopes up. I don't think I'll change my mind."

Brooke thanked her profusely and then ran up to her room where she spent most of her time these days.

Candace was a great advocate of classes for new mothers. Maybe the parents of teens needed them even more.

The house was quiet, almost too quiet, but she couldn't think of anything but her daughter's transformation from loving child to demanding teen. Too restless to settle down after the cookies were done, she wandered through the house until she ended up in front of the bookcase that held the family's memory books. She pulled out a scrapbook that held many of Brooke's early photographs and took it to the couch.

Who was this girl who now challenged her at every turn? Where did she get her stubborn streak? Candace was sure it wasn't from either of her parents. She opened the book and looked at a photo of the tiny, red-faced creature who had brought so much joy to her parents' lives when she was born.

When she came to the pictures taken on the day of Brooke's baptism, she couldn't help but smile. Her daughter had worn a beautiful lace-trimmed white dress, a gift handmade by Dean's mother. It was still packed away in tissue, preserved for Brooke's daughter if she was fortunate enough to have one.

One close-up photo showed her with fine, light hair. Candace remembered how wonderful it felt to brush her cheek against Brooke's head. Touching a baby's soft skin was too pleasurable for words, and everyone who saw their tiny daughter marveled at her flawless complexion.

Another shot showed Brooke, Dean, and his parents, the adults beaming at the camera. She'd taken the picture, and it was slightly crooked, making her smile at her amateur effort. What she wouldn't give to relive that magical day when their baby was received into the church! Unlike many infants, Brooke hadn't cried when the pastor took her in his arms and sprinkled water on her head. Doctors might disagree and say it was only a gas bubble, but Candace was sure her baby had smiled.

It seemed impossible that a baby so perfect could get even more beautiful, but Brooke had. Her fine blonde fuzz grew into springy curls; and the camera loved her, catching her in happy and thoughtful moments.

Finally Candace closed the scrapbook and hugged it close. She could only relive those wonderful days in her memory, but did that mean that her adored daughter was lost to her? Surely Brooke would mature into a kind and loving young woman. They would share the kind of special relationship that Candace had with her mother.

Someday this quarrelsome stranger would laugh with her over their struggles. Meanwhile, Candace could only pray that she was being the mother Brooke needed during her turbulent teen years.

Cesar looked particularly handsome Sunday evening as they prepared to leave for the class at church. He was wearing a navy sweater over a white dress shirt with his best dress slacks. Elena was so happy that he was joining her that she didn't even mind that she would have a shirt to launder, starch, and iron after just a few hours of wear.

They were among the last to arrive at Holy Trinity, and Elena was pleased to see the big turnout. Her good friends Belinda and Troy Boyd were there, and they thought the class was important enough to get a babysitter for their daughter Hayley. There were even a few newcomers, and Pastor Flynn took time at the beginning of the class to be sure everyone knew each other.

The pastor was always cordial to Cesar on those rare family occasions like Izzy's baptism when he went to church. He must have instinctively known that Cesar wasn't a man to be pressured, and he had prayed with her that her husband would come to know the Lord when she brought her concerns to him.

Pastor Flynn was a rather nondescript man, neither young nor old, with thinning hair and a rather long face. He seemed very ordinary until he started speaking. His voice had a compelling quality that made it a pleasure to listen to his sermons, and he was at his best when teaching.

He opened with a prayer and then invited the class to read along from the Bibles he'd provided as he set the tone for their study.

"Reading from Matthew, chapter ten, verses thirty-five to thirty-nine," he said in a melodious voice. "'For I have come to turn a man against his father, a daughter against her mother, a daughter-in-law against her mother-in-law—a man's enemies will be the members of his own household.

"'Anyone who loves his father or mother more than me is not worthy of me; anyone who loves his son or daughter more than me is not worthy of me; and anyone who does not take his cross and follow me is not worthy of me.'"

Elena glanced at Cesar sitting beside her, but his stoic expression didn't give away his thoughts.

"This is a startling passage, is it not?" the pastor asked. "It sounds harsh. It attacks the sanctity of the family. We have every indication that Jesus loved and honored His mother and embraced His brothers as followers. Why, then, would He make such a controversial statement?"

"He was letting His disciples know the high cost of following Him," one of the class members said.

Pastor Flynn beamed, showing everyone that he'd gotten the response he'd hoped for. He spent the rest of the class exploring what it meant to follow Jesus in modern days. Elena was fascinated by his insights, but Cesar sat as immobile as a statue, not once contributing to the discussion. She would rather he ask questions and bring his objections into the open.

They took a short break to enjoy the cookies and coffee that had been provided, and Elena tried to break through her husband's moody silence.

"You're welcome to ask questions, you know. The pastor likes debate," she assured him.

"I don't have any questions," he said.

When the class was over, Cesar was the first to put on his coat and head for the exit with Elena reluctantly in tow. She liked to visit a little after a class and find out what others thought of the lesson.

"Is something wrong?" she asked, although it was obvious he hadn't been impressed by the first session of the class.

"No."

"Cesar," she said when they were alone outside the building, "I know you too well. Why are you upset? I thought it was a good class. Pastor Flynn is a very good teacher."

"I just didn't care for the message."

"The Bible reading?"

"I see the results of broken families every day in my work. I just think it's wrong to put so slight a value on family relationships."

"That wasn't the message the pastor was trying to put across," she argued, hurrying to follow him to the car.

"It was the message I heard."

Elena was dismayed. Had the class put an even deeper gulf between Cesar and the church? Had bringing him with her done more harm than good? She silently prayed that he would hear and believe the Word, but she was afraid it would take a miracle to convince her stubborn husband.

Chapter Sixteen

CANDACE SMILED TO HERSELF AS SHE REPORTED FOR work Monday morning. Brooke was a different person for the rest of Sunday after her mother agreed to think about having boys at her party. In fact, she was so sweet and cooperative that Candace suspected it was another ploy to get her way. At least it made for a pleasant family evening.

Her serene mood was quickly shattered when she came into the Birthing Unit. Riley was there ahead of her looking more harassed than Candace had ever seen her.

"We have a full house, but that's not our main problem," Riley hurriedly explained. "One of the women checked in with a fever. She's too far along to send home, and I'm trying to arrange a room where she can be isolated from our other mothers and babies after she delivers."

"Flu symptoms?" Candace asked with concern.

"We aren't sure yet, but everyone who goes near her will have to wear full protective gear including gowns and masks. Her husband made a bit of a fuss, saying that we're scaring her, but he calmed down when I threatened to have him escorted out of the labor room."

Of all the units in the hospital, none was more vulnerable than theirs, something brought home by this second scare. They'd been fortunate that the first woman tested negative for the flu virus strain they were worried about, but would this case be a false alarm too?

Candace could scarcely imagine the consequences if the epidemic started among the newborns and their mothers. There was so much about the new strain of flu that no one seemed to understand. It was becoming the stuff of nightmares. She was glad that the task force was meeting this evening. It would be a public meeting, so anyone who wanted more information could attend. Maybe they would get some answers then. She trusted Maxine to keep them informed as new information came through the county health office.

The staff all breathed a sigh of relief when the feverish mother gave birth to a healthy, squalling, nine-pound boy. There were no complications, and the newborn and his mother were quickly spirited away to a room better designed to keep them isolated.

The problem didn't end when they left, however. The delivery room had to be thoroughly cleaned, and everything the patient touched had to be sterilized before it was ready for a new patient—and they had two women waiting to use it.

"This is only one possible case of the flu," Riley said. "Imagine what it will be like if we actually have an epidemic. I don't know if the Birthing Unit could continue functioning."

Candace was just as worried as the nurse supervisor. They'd started asking all incoming patients whether they'd had the vaccine, but there always seemed to be a few who had either refused to have a shot or whose doctors hadn't recommended one. And now there was a shortage. The hospital served a large area, not just the town of Deerford, and today it felt like a leaky ship. The basic structure was sound, but the virus could still penetrate their defenses.

Before she went to lunch, Candace scrubbed her hands for several minutes with a strong antibacterial soap. A nurse couldn't allow herself to become paranoid, but the flu scare was making everyone in the unit more conscious of the risk.

Her hands still smelled like the chemicals in the soap when she went into the cafeteria for lunch. James and Anabelle were sitting together at a table near the rear of the room. She was going to spare them the smell clinging to her hands, but James waved her over after she put a serving of vegetable soup and corn bread on her tray.

"Come join us," he said when she approached.

"We heard that you have a sick woman in the Birthing Unit," Anabelle said.

"Sadly, it's true," Candace said as she sat down with them. "She's in isolation now. We can only pray that her son isn't infected. Of course, the tests aren't back. She may not have the flu."

"This is the second scare in your unit, isn't it?" Anabelle asked.

"Afraid so, but the first one didn't prove to be the new strain of flu. We can only hope for negative tests on this one too."

"You'll both be at the task force meeting this evening, won't you?" James asked.

They both agreed that they would.

"We'll confirm the date for a drill," he said.

"We really need firm guidelines," Candace said. "I'm sure we wasted time this morning getting permission to isolate our patient. It's really stressful when we're not sure whether to let a patient give birth in the labor room. We also need stricter rules about who can be with the women in labor and who can visit after the baby is born. The evening supervisor had trouble with one family last week. Two older siblings wanted to see their new sister, but one had a bad runny nose and the other was coughing. The father was angry when his children weren't allowed to come in."

"He wouldn't be too happy if the newborn caught their cold," Anabelle said.

"Some people don't worry about germs and viruses," James said. "They can't see them, so they choose to ignore their existence."

"You'll have to excuse me," Anabelle said, gathering the remains of her lunch as she stood. "I want to call Cameron before I go back to work. He's excited about cooking lessons. He was going to call this morning to see if enough people had signed up for the Happy Heart class."

"Cameron is going to take cooking lessons?" Candace asked.

"I'm afraid we both are. He was quite impressed with the owner of the new shop, the Chef's Corner, but he insisted that I sign up with him. He thinks it will be fun, but he's still a little hesitant, afraid that he'll be the only man in the class. Really, you'd think this was the 1950s. Anyway, it will be worth my time if he learns a healthier way to cook."

"Sounds like fun for both of you," James said.

"I hope so." Anabelle gave them both a broad smile. "Now that I've met Sherry, the owner and teacher, maybe I should go along just to chaperone. She oozes southern charm."

James laughed, and Candace joined in. She didn't know a more devoted couple than the Scotts, unless it was James and Fern. A tiny part of her envied their marital harmony, but she loved them both and wanted nothing but the best for them.

"I did want to ask you something," Candace said as James finished a gelatin dessert. "Brooke is determined to have boys at her birthday party, but she'll only be thirteen. I think she's too young. When did your boys start getting interested in girls?"

James laughed. "My boys share a lot of things with me, but not always that. As far as dating, it hasn't really come up yet. Gideon may be waiting until he finds someone special. Nelson still seems more interested in Scouts and his church activities. But I imagine that can change any time."

"Brooke thinks her party will be a dud if she can't invite boys. I've said no more than once, but she doesn't give up. I've promised to give it some thought, but I still don't think it's a good idea."

"If you don't let her invite boys, she'll think she's really missed something. If you do, maybe they won't come. Or maybe the party won't be as much fun as she expects. It's a hard decision. Remember, forbidden fruit always tastes the sweetest."

"Only you would say that," she said with a soft giggle. She thought of Heath. What would he think about all this? They'd been so busy that there wasn't much time for them to spend alone or even have a coherent conversation. Plus, she wasn't sure she was ready for him to share in her parental decision making. For now, she'd stick with asking her trusted group of friends. "Do you think I should let her have boys?"

"You're the mother," James reminded Candace. "If you strongly object, stick to your original decision, but be sure she knows your reason for saying no. I've found kids are more reasonable if they understand your point of view."

"I wish. I was looking at her baby pictures and remembering what a sweet baby she was. We don't get to keep our babies long, do we?"

"No, but the teen years don't last forever either. If we do our job right, we'll have adult children who do us proud."

"That's the catch—doing my job right."

"I'm sure you'll make the right decision," James said.

Candace wasn't sure, but she realized that she hadn't even asked James how his family was doing.

"How's Fern? Is she still doing as well as she was?"

"Thankfully, yes, but she is sad about losing Sapphire."

"Then the pet detective wasn't able to find her?"

"All I got from her was a crazy plan to knock on every door in town. Even if I had time, I would only annoy a lot of people. My immediate neighbors were a little offended that I would think they had our cat, so I gave up on that. And I really don't want the boys canvassing strangers. It makes their mother nervous, and they need the time for school and other activities."

"I'm sorry you haven't had any success."

"I offered to get Fern a new cat, but she isn't ready yet. She was pretty attached to Sapphire."

"Maybe the pet detective has some other ideas. You have no reason to believe Sapphire isn't alive."

"Maybe," James said, "but all I can think about now are the plans for the hospital drill."

Elena smiled at the picture of four superhero nurses that Izzy had drawn for her. It was hanging on the fridge, held there by a daisy magnet, as she cleaned the kitchen after dinner. If hospital preparedness weren't so important, she would gladly stay home instead of going to the task force meeting.

Rafael made the meeting seem especially important. He was the only one in the family who hadn't had the vaccine. If he did come down with the flu, she wanted him to have the best possible care. That might mean going to Hope Haven.

When she got to the conference room, it was surprisingly crowded. Apparently the small notice in the newspaper had attracted quite a few people not associated with the hospital.

She was the last member of the task force to arrive, but Candace had saved her a seat at the long conference table. So far, the members of the communications committee hadn't been asked to do much, but they had to be prepared in case of a real epidemic.

"Thank you all for coming," James said. "Our first order of business is to confirm the date for the hospital drill. Several of you have been working hard to get ready. If there's no objection, it will be held one week from today."

"That seems awfully soon," Penny said from her seat directly to his left.

"I agree," James said, "but a drill is only valuable if it's held before an actual epidemic."

"Then you're expecting the flu to hit Deerford in the near future?" a woman asked.

Elena turned and recognized her as a reporter for the local paper.

"No," James said emphatically. "We have no reason to believe that, but as long as the possibility exists, Hope Haven should be prepared."

"I heard that you already have one case," a man at the rear said. "Can you confirm that?"

"We have a patient who was admitted with a relatively high fever, but the tests aren't back from the state lab. We're hoping it's a false alarm, but meanwhile, she's in isolation."

"The worst thing the community can do," Maxine spoke up, "is to react with panic to every report of sickness. People do get sick, but that doesn't mean they have the flu."

"Should everyone who gets sick come to the hospital to be checked out?" a gray-haired woman asked.

"No, contact your own physician first if you have suspicious symptoms. Our Emergency Room can't possibly handle every case of the sniffles or sinus congestion," Maxine said.

"What about stomach flu?" the same woman asked.

"Your own doctor should access your condition before you even consider coming to the hospital," Dr. Hamilton said.

"Is this the same flu that killed so many people?" a belligerent voice asked.

"Where is that supposed to have taken place?" Maxine asked in a calm, professional voice.

"I thought you knew that," the man said. "Maybe Africa or Asia or one of those foreign places."

"Flu fatalities are pretty rare," the county health nurse said. "But even seasonal flu can be devastating for people who are in poor health. We're concerned with a special strain that has shown up over the winter, but fortunately most people recovered."

"But not all?" the gray-haired woman asked.

"We're getting off track," Dr. Hamilton said, standing to lend his support to Maxine. "The point is, if we are unfortunate enough to have an epidemic, Hope Haven will be prepared to handle the emergency. But don't come to the hospital for reassurance. Call your family physician. They'll be well informed and prepared to answer any questions you may have about your own health."

He sat down, and Elena was pleased to see that the combined authority of the doctor and the county health nurse had satisfied most of those with questions. James brought up several other points, emphasizing how much cooperation they were getting from other health facilities and community services. A number of retired doctors and nurses had agreed to help out, both during the drill and in a real emergency. The Red Cross was on alert, and local leaders would lend their expertise to the preparedness drill.

Elena looked around at the other members of the task force, and Dr. Weller caught her eye. He winked, and she returned his little grin. It was great to have someone with experience helping out, but she was going to have to get used to doctors who didn't look any older than her son.

Maxine assured everyone that the drill wouldn't interfere with any phase of patient care except optional surgery, which had already been rescheduled to facilitate the preparedness activities.

Looking at her, Elena had a sudden flash of insight, but it faded before she could fully focus on it.

"That went well, don't you think?" Candace asked.

"Yes, very well," she agreed, trying to remember why Maxine had suddenly reminded her of someone else.

As soon as she'd hurried out of the hospital, Elena's mind went back to Cesar. He'd refused to talk about the class, not at breakfast and not during their hasty dinner. He made a point of questioning Rafael about the law enforcement class he was taking and joking with Izzy. She couldn't get him to tell her whether he planned to go next Sunday, but she had a strong suspicion that he wouldn't.

When she left for the task force meeting, he'd settled down to watch the penguin movie with Izzy while Rafael did some assigned reading for his class. Everything might seem normal at their house, but she knew Cesar. He was stewing, and nothing she could say would convince him that the class was about what it meant to follow Christ and not that family wasn't important.

Chapter Seventeen

AFTER THE MEETING CANDACE GOT HOME IN time to kiss her sleepy son good night and remind Brooke that it was nearly her bedtime. She was pleasantly surprised when her daughter meekly agreed to put aside the book she was reading and get ready for bed. Granted that this was sometimes a long process with lots of delays and excuses, but Brooke's change of attitude was more than welcome after a long, hard day at the hospital.

Not only that, she actually was ready to turn out her light in less than fifteen minutes.

"Mommy," she called down the stairs, "will you come say good night to me?"

Candace gladly obliged, remembering how much she used to enjoy reading a story to her daughter at bedtime. She found her snuggled under her quilt, looking younger and more vulnerable than she did during the day.

"Mommy," she said, "do you remember what you promised?"

"Are you talking about your party?"

"Yes, you said you'd think about letting me invite boys."

"I have been thinking," Candace said carefully. "I just don't know if it's best for you."

"It would make me happy. Isn't that a good thing?"

Candace sat beside her on the bed and remembered what James had said about giving children the reason for decisions.

"Sometimes the thing that makes us happy at the moment proves to be a mistake later on." Candace thought about what she'd just said and knew it wouldn't fly. Brooke didn't want to hear vague abstractions. If she couldn't invite boys, she needed to hear a concrete reason. Her mother's worries about growing up too fast wouldn't convince her to give up on the idea.

"Why would it be a mistake?" Brooke sat up and pulled the quilt under her chin.

"You're too young to start dating." Candace braced herself for an explosion but didn't relax when none came.

"I don't want to start dating," Brooke said in a confused voice. "That's not what this is about. Although... when I do start dating, wouldn't it be helpful if I knew more about how boys act? The only boy I really know is Howie, and he acts like a baby most of the time."

When had motherhood gotten so complicated? For a fleeting moment Candace wanted to talk to her own mother and tap into her wisdom, but Janet had made it clear that the party was her problem.

"That's a good point," Candace said. "Can I have a little more time to think about it?"

"Okay," she said. "Just remember, Mother," Brooke said in a pleading voice, as if offering her closing argument, "if I don't have boys at my party, my friends will think I'm a baby."

"Your father always told you not to be one of the sheep. Do you remember that?"

"No, and I don't know what it means."

"It means to think for yourself and do what's right, no matter what your friends do. Sheep will follow a leader without giving a thought to whether they should."

"What if the leader leads them over a cliff?"

"That's the point," Candace said. She said good night and went down to the kitchen where her mother was fixing a cup of tea.

"It's hard to say no to a little angel, isn't it?" her mother asked with a sympathetic grin.

"She's been so sweet and cooperative, I feel mean not agreeing to have boys at the party. It would be easier to say yes and be done with it."

"It always is," Janet said. "Now, would you like a cup of tea? The water is still hot."

Candace sipped tea and talked about her day at the hospital, but Janet was firm about not helping with the decision about the party.

When bedtime came, Candace took her dilemma to the Lord in prayer, beseeching Him for the wisdom to do what was best for her daughter.

Lying wide-eyed under the covers, she tried to come up with a solution. She desperately wished she had someone to help her think this through; once again, she realized she did.

Her mind went again to Heath. He was a kind, understanding man who always took her seriously. He had gone out of his way to befriend both of her children. They loved it when he paid attention to them, and Howie frequently talked about playing games with him. Heath was an honest person too. So why would she be hesitant to let him in on her struggles? She decided she would talk with Heath about it after all. If he supported her decision, she would feel better about it. If he didn't, she would respect that too.

Yet . . . it would be easy to involve Heath in the decision, but would it be right? Her mind felt like the waves of the sea. Her children were so vulnerable since they'd lost their father. They were overly eager to attach themselves to a father figure, but was it in Brooke's best interests? If Candace changed her mind about the party, should she give credit to Heath? If Brooke saw him as a person who could intercede for her, what would her reaction be if things didn't work out? She didn't want her children to face another loss.

She tossed and turned, torn between wanting the support of a man and afraid of the consequences. Above all, she didn't want her children's memories of their father to fade away. Howie was too young to remember him, but Brooke had been daddy's little girl. Candace didn't ever want to betray his memory by letting her daughter forget him.

If her children had been grown and on their own, she would feel free to put her own happiness first. But they were both at vulnerable ages, and every decision she made could have damaging consequences.

Sometimes life was so complicated that she didn't know how to cope.

James was glad to have the public meeting behind him, but there was still a great deal of work to do before the preparedness drill. He got up earlier than usual Tuesday morning. No matter how busy he was at the hospital, he still had a few jobs to do before he went to work.

He made coffee and brought a cup to Fern, preferring that she stay in bed until it was time to see the boys off. Although they routinely made their own breakfasts, she wouldn't dream of letting them leave without a few words of motherly advice.

"Have you thought any more about getting a new cat?" James asked as he perched beside his wife on the edge of the bed.

"I don't feel comfortable getting a replacement for Sapphire," she said thoughtfully. "It would be awful to get attached to another one and then have it disappear too. If we knew for sure what happened to her..."

"I understand," James said.

They talked for a few minutes, and he still had to create a grocery list and go over some paperwork for the house. He hoped the closing on their old house would come soon so he would no longer be responsible for two house payments.

"I won't be right home after work," he said to Fern, "but I'll get here as soon as I can. Do you need anything from the store?"

"Not that I can think of. And don't worry about Sapphire. She always was an independent cat."

He knew she was still hurting, although she tried hard not to show it. Did she still hope that her pet would be found?

After he wrote out a grocery list, he grabbed his checkbook to be sure he had enough money to pay for the food. He skimmed his entries, and one particularly caught his eye. He'd paid a hefty fee to the pet detective, and she really hadn't done a thing to find their cat. As soon as he had a break today, he was going to call her and demand some hands-on help for his money. He wasn't the kind of person who frequently complained, but he didn't like to waste money.

His morning was filled with patient concerns, and whenever he had a free second, someone on the staff had a question about the upcoming drill.

"What do we tell our regular patients?" a nurse on his floor asked.

"Just tell them it's only a drill. We won't disturb anyone needlessly. There will be some commotion on the first floor, but it shouldn't interfere with regular patient care."

He had so many things on his mind that he forgot about the pet detective until he was eating lunch in the cafeteria. The first time he punched in her number on his cell phone, he got the answering machine. He tried again from the staff lounge with more success.

"I'd like to speak to Mimi Zonn," he said to the person who answered.

"May I tell her who's calling?"

"James Bell."

He waited so long that he nearly hung up, but at last the detective came to the phone.

"Let's see," she said. "You've lost your cat, right? How's the search going?"

"It isn't. Going door-to-door doesn't work, never mind that I don't have the time. People either aren't home or they think I'm accusing them of stealing our cat. I expected more help from your agency. If you remember, I paid a substantial fee."

"Let me pull your file and review the case. I'll get back to you."

"Please do," James said, deciding not to mention this call to Fern. He didn't have much hope, regardless of what Mimi Zonn came up with, and he didn't want his wife to have false hopes.

Would he hear from the pet detective again? Even if he did, what could she do at this late date? At least he wanted the satisfaction of knowing that he hadn't totally wasted his money.

Even though she was on James's committee Candace stayed after work to help Anabelle and Maxine review the vaccine inventories in other counties. The results of the statewide survey were pretty much what they'd expected. No one in the area had an adequate supply. Of those who had missed the fall round of inoculations, only a select few would be able to get shots in case of an epidemic.

The new mother with a fever was still in isolation, but the state lab couldn't be rushed when it came to test results. Almost all the doctors and hospitals in central Illinois were sending an unusual number of specimens for analysis.

"I heard the husband's having a fit," Anabelle said. "He wants to take his wife and baby home, but Dr. Hamilton is standing firm. Until the test results come back, we have to treat her as the first victim of a possible epidemic. She's sick enough to be in the hospital, even without the threat of flu."

"Everyone on our floor is edgy," Candace said. "Fortunately, all of our other mothers seem fine, but it's too soon to be sure she hasn't infected any other patients."

As important as their work was, Candace was still eager to leave the community health office on the main floor of the hospital. She'd run into Heath for a few brief moments at noon, and he'd asked her to meet him at the Corner after her shift ended. He was probably waiting for her now.

"Would you mind if I leave?" she asked the other two women. "I did say I'd meet someone after work."

"Run along," Maxine said, closing her laptop and smiling warmly. "I'm grateful you could help out. My office is snowed under with work. I appreciate so much what the task force is doing, and that certainly includes the two of you. If we do have an epidemic, I'm sure we'll be as well or better prepared than any county in the state."

"That's really nice to hear," Anabelle said.

Candace left and hurried to meet Heath. She walked across the street as a chilly rain slid off her rain hat and soaked her feet. The promise of early spring had given way to cold, soggy weather. Were people more vulnerable to the flu when the weather was damp and unpleasant? She didn't know the answer but prayed it wasn't so.

She still hadn't decided whether to mention Brooke's party to him. It was her decision whether to let boys come, but it would be nice if he agreed with her. Sometimes being a parent was so lonely, even with her mother to help her. It was good that Janet never tried to second-guess decisions about the children, but sometimes Candace needed to feel less alone.

Heath was sitting in one of the booths, facing the door and toying with a cup of coffee. His face lit up with a broad smile when he saw her.

"I'm sorry to keep you waiting," she said, shedding her wet coat and hat and bundling them beside her on the broad seat.

"I don't mind waiting for you," he said with a wink. "What can I get you?"

"I'd love some hot tea." She let out a long, relaxing exhale and settled into the booth.

He gestured at a waitress who didn't seem to be doing anything in the nearly deserted diner and then they talked about their day until she left a pot of hot water and an assortment of foil-wrapped tea bags on their table.

"I wonder if I can run something past you," Candace said to Heath, deciding to mention the party because it was so comforting to sit with him in the cozy little diner. "I have a real dilemma with Brooke."

"I'll do anything I can to help," he assured her. "What's the problem?"

"You know she's turning thirteen. We have a party planned at the Y for the Saturday after her birthday. Now she wants to invite boys, and I'm not sure she's old or mature enough. It's become a real issue between us. I don't know whether I'm being too strict."

"I know that you only want what's best for her." He stared at her with his vivid blue eyes, and she warmed to the sincerity in his voice.

"But am I being overly protective?" She began fidgeting with a tea bag wrapper on the table. "Do you think I should change my mind and let her invite boys?"

He leaned forward and linked his fingers with hers. "I honestly don't know. But I do know I love you."

Candace loved hearing the words. Yet they still made her feel slightly anxious. She loved him too, but it was overwhelming to say the least. She smiled and continued, "I know most of her friends, but I have no idea who the boys are."

"If you don't let her invite them, maybe she'll build them up in her imagination to be romantic heroes. It might make her more interested."

James had mentioned something similar about forbidden fruit. "I can't see anything romantic about the awkward boys I see outside the school," she said with a chuckle, "but then, I'm a long way from thirteen."

Heath released her hands and took a sip of his coffee. "You're worried that you're a bad mother if you say no."

"Something like that."

"Candace, you couldn't be bad if you tried. Someday Brooke will realize what a wonderful mother she has."

"I hope so, but she's going to be difficult if I say no."

"Tell you what. Let's go out tonight. Should I pick you up at seven? We'll have dinner and talk some more. That way I'll have time to think about it. You can't spring a big decision like that on an old bachelor without giving him some time to mull it over."

Candace felt a telling catch in her throat. She still couldn't believe that she was being given a second chance at love with this wonderful man. She'd vowed not to compare him to Dean, but he had an innate goodness that reminded her of her late husband's kindness and integrity.

"I'd like that," she said. "Please come in and say good night to Howie. He thinks the world of you."

"Will do, and don't worry. No matter what you decide, Brooke will understand someday."

He took her hands again, giving them a reassuring squeeze.

"I'll walk you to your car. I just happen to have an umbrella with me."

His umbrella sheltered her from the rain, but his growing love was a much greater comfort. She wished that she could accept it unconditionally, but she wasn't a young girl who had only herself to think of.

God had given her two precious children to fill the void in her life when Dean passed away. She wanted to be the best possible mother, even if it meant accepting the emptiness in her heart, but it was terribly hard to know what was right and what was wrong for Brooke and Howie.

Chapter Eighteen

"WE'RE IN," CAMERON SAID BEFORE ANABELLE COULD get her coat off after work.

"In what?" she asked absentmindedly, her mind still full of the possibility of a flu epidemic.

"The cooking class. Sherry called. Her Happy Heart class is a hit. She has eleven people signed up, three of them men."

"Then you really don't need me to go with you," Anabelle said, wanting nothing more than to kick off her shoes and have a relaxing cup of herbal tea.

"Hey, Annie, we're in this together. You're the one who wants me to eat more healthy food. You're not going to back out on me now, are you?"

"Not if you really want me to go with you," she said, smiling to hide how reluctant she was to add one more thing to her busy schedule. "When do the classes begin?"

"Tomorrow. Sherry asked if that was too soon, but I told her the sooner, the better. She wouldn't tell me what our first recipe will be, but she gave me a hint: Georgia's favorite fruit. I'm pretty sure that means something with peaches."

"Good guess," she said, trying to muster up enthusiasm to match her husband's. "What time does the class start?"

"Five o'clock. We're supposed to bring hearty appetites because we'll be eating whatever we cook. I can't believe it, but I'm actually looking forward to Sherry's lessons."

"Meanwhile, how about a big salad for dinner? We have all the ingredients, and I can boil a couple of eggs for our protein."

"I'm a step ahead of you," he said beaming with satisfaction. "Since this is our last dinner before we learn to cook healthy food, I got a chuck roast this morning. It's been cooking in the Crock-Pot all day. I threw in onions, potatoes, salt, and some other seasoning. It should be tender enough to fall apart by now."

"Oh, Cam, I thought our dinner at the restaurant was your last fling."

"That doesn't count because we ate out. This will be the last time I can fix anything I want. I went easy on the dessert though, just bakery pound cake with vanilla ice cream and caramel sauce. I thought of that combination myself."

Anabelle's shoulders drooped, and she was at a loss for words. Would cooking classes be enough to convince her husband to change his eating habits? Now that he had lots of time to think about food, he wanted to eat far more than he had during his working days.

She went upstairs to freshen up, dreading the meal to come. Watching her husband consume rich food ruined her own appetite. If it wouldn't hurt his feelings, she would gladly settle for tea and soda crackers instead of the dinner he'd prepared.

"It will do you good to get out," Janet said as she zipped the back zipper on Candace's light blue jersey dress.

"Work takes me away so much. I feel guilty going out to dinner on a school night." She smoothed down her dress and slipped a long silver chain over her head. "Anyway, I'm going to feel silly in this dress if Heath shows up in jeans and a polo shirt. I should change into my black slacks and a sweater."

"Nonsense. There's nothing wrong with dressing up a bit. It's nice to see you in something besides scrubs and everyday clothes."

"Well, thank you for putting the kids to bed. I know it's always hard for Howie to settle down after he sees Heath."

"It would be good for him to have a male teacher," Janet said, speaking as a retired media specialist in the school system. "I don't see that happening for a couple of years. Fifteen, twenty years ago we actually had a man teaching kindergarten. The kids adored him. He was like the Pied Piper. Unfortunately, he left for a better paying job in the private sector."

Candace scarcely listened. They'd lived together since Dean's death, more than long enough for her to hear all her mother's stories. What she needed was to hear that it was all right to put herself first by going out on a school night, but she wasn't a child who could be easily reassured anymore.

Alone in the bathroom, she brushed on her favorite coral lip gloss. It went well with the coppery highlights in her brown bob, but she didn't like it with her dress. She vigorously wiped it off and applied a pale pink. She didn't like it any better, but she was out of time and just a little embarrassed for fussing with makeup. She wasn't a teenage girl getting ready for her first date.

In fact, she was toying with the idea of canceling. She'd had a long day, and she hated to miss reading Howie's bedtime story.

The doorbell rang, and Howie tore out of his room and raced down the stairs to answer it.

"Hi, Sport. Give me five," Heath said, holding out his hand so Howie could smack his open palm against it.

Brooke's dignity wouldn't allow her to join the race to the door, but she went halfway down the stairs and hung on the banister where she could see Heath.

"Hi, Brooke," he called out when he saw her.

"Can you play a game with me?" Howie asked. "I don't have to go to bed yet."

"Not tonight," Heath said. "Next time we'll have a marathon."

"That's when you play lots and lots of games in a row, isn't it?"

"Right, but it's too late for that tonight. Your mother hasn't had her dinner yet."

"We had hot dogs," Howie said. "Grammy puts sauerkraut on hers, but I hate it."

"I'm not too crazy about it either. I like lots of ketchup and mustard."

"Yuck, I don't like mustard. It's too yellow," Howie said turning up his nose.

"Shall we go?" Heath asked when Candace appeared, automatically going to the closet and getting out her good wool coat.

He was wearing a camel hair sports coat and dark slacks with a turtleneck, but he hadn't bothered with an outer coat. She couldn't help but notice how trim and agile he was, and part of her wanted his strong arms around her, sheltering her from all the setbacks of everyday life.

"Ready?" he asked with a winning smile.

"All ready." She bent and kissed the top of Howie's head and waved good night to Brooke, who was still hovering on the stairs.

She was getting way ahead of herself, but Heath had shown that he wanted them to have a closer relationship. If he proposed, how would she answer? What if things didn't work out and her children had to lose another father figure? Would it be better to end things now?

These thoughts were new and a little frightening. There was no question that she loved Heath, but first and foremost, she had to think of her children.

Heath lifted Howie and swung him around to his delighted squeals.

"I won't be late," she said to her mother. "Thanks for putting the kids to bed."

"No problem," Janet said, although they both knew that it wouldn't be easy to settle Howie down after he saw Heath.

He surprised her by driving to the Heritage House.

"I wasn't expecting to come here," she said.

"You looked a bit down today. I thought it might cheer you up."

"That's sweet of you," she said.

The Heritage House was the place where people came for special events. She hoped Heath didn't have any surprises planned. She felt weary and torn between her feelings for him and what was best for her children.

Tuesday was a slow night, so they were the only ones in a room that had once been the parlor. Candace liked the period pictures on the wall, especially a portrait of a lovely young woman in an ornate metal frame with rounded glass, but she didn't have much appetite for the elaborate meals that were served there. She ordered a lamb chop with vegetables and hoped it would be a modest-sized entrée. Heath ordered blackened swordfish, which struck her as an odd thing to serve in the middle of Illinois, far from any ocean.

In fact, everything about this evening seemed out of kilter. They'd gone out together many times, but usually not on a weeknight. Maybe her fatigue was catching up with her, but she had a hard time keeping her attention focused on his conversation.

"You look done in," he said sympathetically after she'd picked away at the salad that came with her dinner.

"Things have been worrisome at work," she said, although she knew that wasn't her reason for feeling tired.

They talked about Hope Haven throughout the meal, and Candace found it relaxing to focus on their mutual commitment to good health care. Both of them passed on dessert and were enjoying cups of decaf coffee when Heath brought up the subject of Brooke.

"Your little girl is growing up fast," he mused. "She's getting as pretty as her mother."

"Too fast," Candace said. "I really don't think she's ready to have a party with boys."

"I remember my first boy-girl party," he said with a grin. "I was in middle school. I think it was a girl's birthday. Anyway, it was in her recreation room."

"How did it go?"

"I'd classify it as a minor disaster. The boys stood around at one end of the room and the girls at the other. Finally her older brother threw a basketball at us, and all the boys trooped outside and chose up sides for a game. If the girls watched us, we didn't notice."

"I suppose that could happen if Brooke invited boys," she said thoughtfully.

"I have a suggestion if you want to hear it," he said.

"What?" she asked, curious about whether he had a solution.

"Let Brooke invite the boys. I'll help chaperone. If there's any problem, I'll be there to help."

"I don't know."

"You did say it's at the Y, didn't you? If things go wrong, I can always get the boys to shoot baskets or something."

"It's a lot to ask of you." She let the idea set in.

"I'll enjoy it. Most of the kids I see have broken bones," he said with a laugh. "About Brooke's party, if you really don't want to invite boys, then that's what you should do. But I think the two of us could handle it without any problems, and you'll make your daughter very happy."

"There is that," Candace said, feeling convinced against her will. "But if I stand firm, she will understand someday. Are you sure that you want to give up a Saturday evening to chaperone?" She was half convinced, but something still didn't seem right.

"I won't be giving up anything. You'll be there, and it will give me a chance to see teens in action. My memories of those days are getting hazy."

"You remember your first boy-girl party."

"Only because it didn't go well."

"Suppose I say yes, and Brooke's party doesn't live up to expectations. I hate to see her disappointed. She's looked forward to this party for so long."

He shook his head, and a shadow of sadness passed over his features. "I'm no child psychologist, but I have read that children should experience small disappointments and frustrations so they can better cope with large ones when they're adults."

"Yes, I've heard that somewhere. I guess no mother can protect her children from all the bad things in the world."

"No, but you can teach them to cope."

What he said made sense. Maybe she was making too much out of a simple party. After all, it was only a couple hours, and Brooke would be so happy if she said yes to boys.

An old saying she'd heard ages ago floated through her mind: A man convinced against his will is of the same opinion still. Well, she was a woman and more importantly the mother of a soon-to-be teen. Maybe Heath was right. It might be better to let Brooke have the party her way, even if it didn't meet her expectations.

"You have a job chaperoning," she said as they stood to leave.

"If it helps you, I'm happy," he murmured, putting his hand on the small of her back.

She didn't want their time together to end, but she still had doubts about the party. Her confusion didn't end when Heath walked her to the front door and gently pressed his lips against her forehead before saying good night.

Brooke should have been in bed when Candace got home, but instead she was on the steps in almost the same place she'd been sitting when Heath came for Candace.

"Did you have fun?" her daughter asked as Candace hung up her coat.

"We had a nice dinner." She wasn't sure it counted as fun, especially since Heath had convinced her to change her mind about the party. "I have news for you."

"I was hoping!"

"Why?"

"You'll be mad at me."

"Brooke, what's up?"

"I called Heath."

"And?"

"Nothing much. I mentioned that I wanted to have a boy-girl party for my birthday. Did he convince you?"

Candace felt strangely double-crossed. "Brooke, I'm not happy that you did that."

"You know how badly I want a mixed party. My friends can't understand why you won't let me."

Candace sat beside her daughter on the step, at a loss to know how to handle the situation.

"I was going to tell you that you could have boys," she said in an unhappy voice.

"Thank you, thank you, thank you!"

"Wait! I *was* going to change my mind, but you shouldn't have called Heath."

"I know, but I was desperate. I'm not even sure some of my friends will come if it's just us girls."

"That doesn't excuse going behind my back."

"I told you the truth. You always say you won't punish us if we tell the truth."

"I expect more from you. You're not a baby anymore."

"I'm sorry. I didn't know you'd be mad."

"Oh, Brooke." She hugged her daughter close and tried to think through the situation. Part of her was glad Brooke would even let Candace envelop her in a hug.

"All right, you can invite a reasonable number of boys, but I want to see your list first," she said in a cautious voice. "And you have to make a promise."

"Anything!"

"You have to promise that you'll never go behind my back like that again. Not with your grandmother and not with Heath."

"I promise. I didn't know that I was doing such a bad thing."

"Now go to bed."

"Thank you, Mommy!"

Brooke hugged her and dashed up to her room, her fuzzy yellow robe flopping behind her.

Candace sat for a long time, head in her hands, trying to sort out her feelings.

Chapter Nineteen

ELENA'S CO-WORKERS WERE ON EDGE WEDNESDAY morning, with good reason. They were still processing their roles in the preparedness drill, and so far there was no news about the woman in isolation. Everyone agreed that she must be seriously ill to stay in the hospital that long, but was she the first victim of a dreaded epidemic? Elena tried to stay optimistic, but it was difficult when everyone around her was worried.

"I heard that she has swollen glands and a strange rash," one of the younger nurses said to Elena at the nurses' station.

"Next people will be saying she has bubonic plague," Elena said, feeling cross because the rumors were getting worse with each retelling.

"Do you think—"

"Absolutely not!" Elena looked around, relieved that no patients were wandering the corridor within hearing distance.

"Please, think of how our patients will feel if they hear wild rumors like that."

"I'm sorry," the young nurse said. "I didn't think about that."

Elena wanted to wring her hands in frustration, but maybe it was good that she was on the communications committee. Surely an important part of her job was to stop harmful gossip.

At least she had her regular Bible class to look forward to this evening. Cesar was never enthusiastic about having her go to it, but he didn't make a fuss anymore. She didn't know whether he would ever share her faith in the Lord, but at least he respected her decision to be active in church.

So far he hadn't said more about the Sunday evening class. He didn't want to talk about it and turned a deaf ear when she tried to explain that the first lesson hadn't been antifamily. It was just a measure of the commitment early apostles had to make to spread the word.

She went to the cafeteria for lunch, alert for more rumors as staff members talked at the tables. Fortunately the scattered bits of conversation that she caught involved other topics. She didn't like the idea of heading up the rumor police, but she thought health care workers should hold themselves to higher standards than the uninformed public.

When she got home, Cesar was already there, sitting alone at the kitchen table with a cup of coffee.

"Where are the kids?" she asked.

"I sent Rafael to the store with Izzy to get one of those chickens that are already roasted and some deli salads. Thought it would give you a break from cooking for a change. I imagine you're going to Bible group tonight."

"Yes, that was nice of you to take care of dinner."

He shrugged, and she knew him well enough to know that there was more than consideration behind the gesture.

"I wanted to talk to you."

She guessed as much.

"I dropped in on Pastor Flynn during my break."

"Oh, did you have a nice visit?" She held her breath wondering why he did that.

"I wouldn't call it nice or a visit. He said the same thing you did about that lesson. I guess he convinced me that the church strongly supports the family."

"Is that all you talked about?"

"More or less. At least the man didn't pressure me to come to church."

Elena knew the pastor was a wise man. "Is that all you wanted to tell me?"

So far he hadn't said anything that couldn't be said in front of their son and granddaughter.

"I guess."

"Okay."

But it wasn't okay. Cesar could be a hard man to read, and he didn't talk about feelings very often.

"That doesn't mean I intend to go through the whole series of classes. I only went because I wanted to spend more time with you."

"I appreciate that."

She wanted Cesar to get down on his knees and pray with her, but she knew that wasn't going to happen, not until he truly accepted the Lord as his Savior.

The kitchen door exploded inward, and Izzy rushed over to give her a hug.

"Daddy let me get salad with little marshmallows in it," she happily announced.

"Here's dinner," Rafael said, close on her heels. "The chicken is in an insulated sack, so I think we're good to go."

"I'll set the table," Elena said. "You two go hang up your coats and wash your hands."

"I'd better do the same," Cesar said without looking at her.

As she laid out their ready-made supper, Elena tried to pin down exactly what Cesar had been telling her. Was he less upset about the message in the Scriptures now that he'd talked to the pastor? Surely he must know that their church was very family oriented. Maybe he wanted to soften the blow when he refused to go to more classes.

Or maybe he was confused about how he felt and wanted her to say something that would help him sort out his reasons for rejecting the faith. If so, she had failed him, but she didn't know what else she could say or do to change his mind.

She silently prayed that her example would someday lead him to believe. Beyond that, she didn't know what else she could do.

Anabelle arrived home on Wednesday with more than enough time to change her clothes for the cooking class. Dr. Hamilton had asked her to meet with him after her shift ended. He wanted to go over some details of the drill that involved the Cardiac Care Unit, and she was always happy to cooperate with him. Not only was his wife a good friend and quilting companion, the doctor had given care and support when their daughter Kirstie was severely injured in a bicycle accident at age ten. He had taken the essential step of amputating her leg, but he'd also guided the family through her recovery. When he requested something, Anabelle never thought of refusing.

"You just made it," Cameron said, looking pretty spiffy for a cooking class.

He was wearing a new blue-and-white-striped shirt he'd gotten for Christmas and, unless she was mistaken, he had ironed his tan cotton slacks.

"I'll hurry and change. Aren't you afraid you'll stain your new shirt? You don't know what we'll be fixing."

"Remember, Sherry provides aprons as part of the fee. Now you'd better hurry. Don't forget to wear shoes with toes. Don't want you dropping something and breaking a toe if you wear sandals."

"It is March," she said.

Anabelle wanted nothing more than to soak in a hot tub and let the day's tensions seep out of her pores. She was a good cook and didn't expect to learn anything of interest in the class, but she wasn't doing this for herself. If Cam became enthusiastic about healthy cooking, it was worth as much of her time as it took.

She quickly changed into an old pair of navy slacks and a yellow oxford shirt with sleeves she could roll up. Cam was wearing his navy peacoat and holding her dog-walking jacket when she came downstairs.

"Did you feed Sarge?" she asked, checking her watch to see that they had plenty of time to drive into town.

"An hour ago, and I put him out and brought him back in. The stove and the lights are all off, so there's nothing for you to check before we go."

"We're going to be the first ones there," she said.

"Better than being last. It will give us time to look around in the store. Some of our kitchen stuff is pretty old. Look at the roasting pan that used to be your mother's. It has so many dings it looks like it was used for target practice."

"We don't need a pan that large for the two of us."

"You might need one for holiday dinners. Think about how our family has expanded."

"For today, let's just concentrate on learning to cook more sensibly."

She was right about being early. When they got to the Chef's Corner, they had nearly half an hour to wait before the class started. Cameron entertained himself by picking out a skillet that was guaranteed to last fifty years and a set of cooking utensils with sleek chrome handles that duplicated everything she had in a drawer at home. He insisted that nonstick surfaces were essential to a good cook. She tried not to groan out loud.

Finally the class members were all assembled at designated spots along a counter. One of the men, Barry, was a boyish-looking husband who was struggling to grow a beard with limited success. The class seemed to be his idea, since his wife snapped her gum and looked bored about being there. The other man was, politely put, huge, and Anabelle suspected that he was there because his wife, a tiny little woman with white hair and a youthful face, had insisted.

The other two women were probably in their fifties and seemed more interested in talking to each other than meeting the others or listening to the instructor. In fact, Sherry had to ask them to stop talking so she could begin the class, although she did it with good-natured courtesy.

There were a total of eight in the class, apparently enough to launch it, although Cam had been expecting the maximum number of eleven. Anabelle wished that the kitchen had stools to sit on during the lesson. She'd already been on her feet most of the day.

"I have a real treat for you today," Sherry said after passing out white aprons that tied around their waists. She was wearing an adorable pink one with embroidered butterflies over a dress with frilly ruffles instead of sleeves. The teacher definitely qualified as the cutest. Anabelle wiggled her toes in her sturdy walking shoes and hoped the class didn't last too long.

"A sweet man who works in the supermarket meat department managed to get enough fresh tilapia for one of my favorite dishes."

"What's tilapia?" the gum-chewing young woman asked.

"It's a wonderful fish that came here from the Mediterranean and Africa. Now it's outstripped trout as the most popular fish to farm. Florida has outdoor ponds, but it can be grown anywhere in a system of filtered tanks. You surely do have a taste treat coming. The mild flavor is just about perfect for all kinds of recipes. Anyone on a heart-healthy diet should make the acquaintance of all kinds of fish, and this one is a good starter."

Anabelle gave her credit for being well prepared. Everyone had a dishwasher-safe plastic cutting board with a generous sheet of plastic under it. Sherry went down the counter passing out disposable gloves, sharp knives, and scraping tools and then laid a whole fish on every board.

"Yuck!" the young wife said. "It's blue."

"Just listen, Hope," her husband said.

"This thing is enough to make me become a vegetarian," she said, backing a few feet away from the counter.

"Just like people, they come in different colors: red, black, blue. One's as tasty as the others," Sherry said cheerfully, apparently not at all disturbed by criticism.

"What are we going to do with these?" one of the older women asked. "They're not cleaned."

"Chefs worth their salt have to know how to clean and prepare their proteins. This will be fun once you get the knack."

Anabelle didn't share her optimism. In fact, she very much wanted to shove hers over to Cam and let him do the messy part.

"Now this is the part of the class where you'll be tempted to tune me out," Sherry said, "but it's terribly, terribly important."

She gave a short lecture on how to tell if fish were fresh and then went on to emphasize how important it was to wash utensils, cutting surfaces, and hands with hot soapy water after processing raw fish. Anabelle thoroughly approved of her advice even though she disliked cleaning fish. Cam was lapping up every word she said the way Sarge drank his water after a good run. She sighed and willed the woman to get on with it.

The young woman and the talkative pair went about cleaning the fish with noisy protests, making Anabelle even more determined to be businesslike, no matter how she disliked the job. She did learn how to remove the small pin bones in the fillet, useful information if she ever wanted to debone another tilapia—which was unlikely.

"I like to marinate fresh fish in a citrus juice. Today I've chosen pineapple juice. Because we have to move right along, we can only leave the tilapia in the fridge for about thirty minutes. If I did this at home, I'd allow at least an hour, but I know you folks are hungry."

When all the fillets were sealed in a plastic bag of juice and stowed in a big metal bowl, they cleaned their workstations.

"Now for something really fun," Sherry said. "I'm going to teach y'all to make southern-style salsa. Guess what the main ingredient will be?"

The group was unanimously unresponsive. Anabelle didn't think that boded well for the success of the class, but Sherry cheerfully continued.

"Peaches, of course! I am so sorry that I couldn't get fresh Georgia peaches, but I did thaw some from my own freezer. I always go a little wild when they're in season."

The class set about making salsa with a great deal of enthusiasm compared to the fish lesson. Anabelle had never made her own, but now that she knew how easy it was, she would definitely do it again. Sherry's recipe included chopped cilantro and minced jalapeño pepper, two ingredients Anabelle had never used. It also had a tablespoon of oil, a dash of lime juice, diced bell peppers, and chopped red onion. She left the salt out, although it only called for half a teaspoon. One of the reasons for taking the class was to show Cam that he could do without a lot of salt.

"You can make up your own recipe when you know the basics," Sherry said. "Sometimes I add cucumber or a hint of mint or ginger. You can also add tomato."

"I thought all salsa was made from tomatoes," Hope said.

"Well, honey, I hope you get all kinds of new ideas from my classes," Sherry said.

They let their small bowls of salsa sit so the flavors could blend while Sherry took their fish from the fridge.

"They all look alike," Hope complained. "How do I know I'm getting mine back?"

"These will be so delicious that it won't matter a lick," their teacher said.

Was she naturally this cheerful, or did she have to practice in front of a mirror? Anabelle reminded herself again why she was there.

"I like to grill these outside after your horrid Midwestern weather gets better," she said, demonstrating how to add lime-butter and seasonings to the fillets. "Now remember where you put your tilapia on the broiling pan. That way you'll get to eat the one you seasoned."

To his credit, Cam avoided the saltshaker and covered his with the special seasoning Sherry recommended. Anabelle could only hope his newfound enthusiasm for healthy cooking Sherry-style would carry over to meals at home.

When the fish was done, the teacher added small portions of steamed sticky brown rice to their plates, and they all went to a table at the rear to taste-test their tilapia and peach salsa.

"Not bad," Cam said. "In fact, I'd give it an A-plus."

Sherry giggled her thanks, and Hope slid her fish onto her husband's plate. Anabelle was as grateful for the chair as she was for the meal.

On the way home, she listened to Cameron rave about the class.

"I guess you want to go again," she said with resignation.

She was a health care professional. This was a small price to pay to keep her husband healthy, wasn't it?

Chapter Twenty

COLD RAIN HAD REDUCED THE SNOW OUTSIDE TO dirty patches, but Elena felt as if she were pushing a huge snowball uphill. Rumors about the woman in isolation were everywhere, and people were edgy about the possibility of an epidemic. As hard as she tried to stop the staff in her own unit from repeating versions of the story, some still persisted in believing that the patient was infected with a dangerous strain of flu.

Her job on the task force was to help with communications, but she felt defeated by the rumors. She understood that people were worried. How could they not be when every unit was preparing for the drill? She also knew that no good could come of panic. They were trained professionals and should be concentrating on their roles in a real disaster, not speculating about a potential crisis that might prove to be a false alarm.

When Maxine left a message at the nurses' station requesting that Elena meet with her after work, she felt relieved. Maybe the county health nurse would have some ideas about controlling rumors.

As usual, one of her first priorities of the day was checking on the coma patient. She always talked to her, hoping that words might penetrate the cloud over her mind. Unless she woke up soon or someone came forward to identify her, she would be moved from Hope Haven to a long-term care facility as a ward of the state. Elena prayed that the kind-faced woman wouldn't be lost in the system. Surely someone somewhere was missing her.

She felt unusually fatigued when it was time to leave the floor for the day. Her job working with critical patients was always demanding, but her weariness went deeper. Things seemed to be spiraling out of control in the hospital, and she couldn't get Cesar out of her mind either. He couldn't complain when she used her free time to make a dance costume for Izzy, but his resentment seemed to simmer just below the surface. She wanted to spend more time with him, but her busy life kept interfering. His job involved overtime, so why did he expect her to be available whenever he had free time?

When she got to the community health room only minutes after her shift ended, she found Maxine alone, sitting in front of her laptop computer with a vacant look on her usually animated features.

"You look as if you just received bad news," Elena said, shutting the door behind her. "Have the test results come back for our potential flu victim?"

"No, not yet. I understand that the state labs are overrun with work. Meanwhile, the patient is off the respirator and asking for her baby."

"One rumor said that the father was allowed to take the infant home, but I don't know what to believe anymore. You'd think the plague was loose in the hospital. Isn't there anything we can do about the stories that are circulating?"

"I'm using the hospital's online resources to refute every rumor I've heard. That's why I wanted to see you. You're in a much better position than I am to know what staff members are saying. If you wouldn't mind working with me..." Her voice trailed off.

As a nurse Elena didn't like her pale color or the redness around her eyes.

"Are you all right?" she asked with concern.

"Oh, don't worry. I don't have any flu symptoms. I'm just worried sick about my sister. We usually talk at least once a week and send e-mails back and forth on a regular basis. I haven't heard from her in weeks, and it really worries me. It's not at all like her to drop out of sight."

"Maybe she's busy at work or with her family," Elena suggested, trying to reassure her.

"Jeanette never married, and I'm her closest family member. She's quite a talented artist. In fact, she makes her living illustrating children's books and teaching an occasional art class. I'm afraid we don't always see eye to eye on some things though. Lately she's taken jobs house-sitting because she hasn't gotten as many contracts as she'd like from publishers. I wanted her to visit us for a while instead of staying alone in strange houses, but Jeanette can be pretty stubborn."

"I know about stubborn," Elena said, pursing her lips and thinking about the men in her family.

"She insisted on watching a house somewhere in the Deerford area, but she never told me the people's name or the address. I was sure she'd send me an e-mail, maybe arrange for us to see each other while she's so close."

"She never did?" Elena had a thought floating on the edge of her consciousness, but she couldn't quite bring it into focus.

"No, I've sent her several e-mail messages every day and tried to call her cell phone number. No response. She never stays angry long, and it's totally unlike her not to let me know where she is. I'm really worried that something has happened to her. I thought of calling the police, but she would be terribly upset if I checked up on her that way. Still, it's been too long. Something isn't right. I've been e-mailing the friends I know, even her main publisher, but no one seems to know where she is."

Elena was wringing her hands without realizing it, adding things up in her mind until she was almost certain that she knew where Maxine's sister was. But she had to be sure before she delivered the bad news.

"Do you have a picture of your sister?"

"I have an old one of the two of us in my billfold, but why do you ask?" The worry lines in her forehead seemed to get deeper.

"Please, can I see it?"

Elena didn't know whether to hope that she was right or hope that she was wrong.

"All right."

Maxine sorted through a small stack of photos crammed into a compartment of her billfold, finally pulling out a creased and faded shot of two women.

"She looks a lot like you," Elena said, staring at the picture with growing dread. How was she going to break the terrible news to this sweet woman?

"She's only two years older. When we were young, we liked to dress in the same clothes, only in different colors. Once in a while, a stranger would ask if we were twins; but I don't think we really looked that much alike."

"Maxine, I don't know how to tell you this . . ." Elena began.

She handed the picture back, dreading the words that had to be said. As often as she dealt with worried and grieving people in her job, she was finding it much harder to give bad news to someone she liked and admired.

"Do you know something about my sister?"

"I'm afraid so. I'm pretty sure she's a patient in ICU."

Maxine stood and came around the table to stand in front of Elena, making it even harder for her to tell her about the unidentified patient.

"It's not good," she said, groping for a way to break the terrible news.

"Tell me."

"We have a patient in a coma. She was walking along a road near Deerford when a vehicle swerved toward her. The paramedics who took the call believe that she ran to the side to avoid being hit and fell down a steep incline. She suffered severe head trauma."

Maxine's eyes were swimming with tears, but she insisted on going directly to the room where her sister might be.

"You're not sure? She didn't have identification?"

"No, but I've been trying to figure out why her face seemed so familiar."

"I have to see your patient."

Elena saw the distress in Maxine's face and posture.

"You could be wrong. Jeanette has a lot of friends. She may be staying with someone who doesn't have a computer. Or hers might have broken down. They don't last forever, you know."

Elena followed her to the elevator, her heart heavy. She should have figured out why the patient's features seemed so familiar before this. She didn't know whether to hope that she was wrong for Maxine's sake or pray that she was right for the patient's.

She put her hand on Maxine's shoulder as they went into the room, but neither words nor touch could cushion the shock when she looked down at the bed.

"It's Jeanette," she said in a hoarse voice. "How long?"

"A little over two weeks."

"Wasn't she carrying *anything* to identify her?"

"No, her things are here in the patient locker." She took out the plastic hospital bag that held everything that had been found on her person.

"I recognize these running shoes," Maxine said. "They're her favorite brand. Once we had to look all over the mall in Peoria to find a new pair her size. And she had sweats just like these."

She dropped the possessions and sat on the edge of the bed, taking her sister's limp hand in hers.

"Jeanette," she said over and over in a soft, sad voice. "What do the doctors say? Will she ever wake up?"

"There's always hope." Elena said the words but had a hard time believing them herself. "They just don't know."

"If she doesn't—"

Elena anticipated her question. "Dr. Hamilton has been looking for long-term care," she said softly.

"My goodness," Maxine said almost under her breath, "how could this happen? If I hadn't found her, she would have been warehoused as a ward of the state. I don't believe that she'll never come out of this. I can't!"

"I believe that the Lord answers prayers," Elena said. "I've prayed for your sister since her accident. I'm only sorry that I didn't connect her to you sooner. I'm not giving up on her. I'm sure you're not going to either."

She stayed and prayed with Maxine, giving her all the comfort her faith and her profession could muster. It was nearly six o'clock before she'd notified Dr. Hamilton and the nursing staff that their coma patient was no longer a Jane Doe. Maxine's husband joined her at the bedside, and Elena quietly left them.

The rumors circulating in the hospital weren't good, but they'd brought Elena to Maxine when she most needed her. She went home, realizing she hadn't called to say she'd be late.

"Where were you?" Izzy asked, throwing herself at Elena's legs the minute she stepped into the house.

"Something came up at the hospital, sweetheart," she said, scooping her granddaughter into her arms.

"The pizza man is coming," she said, slipping away. "I ordered plain cheese. Daddy likes icky stuff on his."

"Phones not working, Mama?" Rafael teased, making the same comment she'd said to him many times.

Cesar was leaning against the kitchen counter, arms folded across his chest.

"Your mother does important work," he reprimanded his son. "If she's late home, she must have a good reason."

He walked over and put his arm around her shoulders just as the front doorbell rang.

"Pizza man!" Izzy shouted excitedly. "You said I could pay him, Daddy."

Rafael followed her to the door to help with the transaction, but Cesar and Elena stayed where they were.

"You didn't stay just for a meeting," he said. "I can see it in your face."

"The coma patient has a sister, Maxine Newman, the county health nurse. I just put two and two together, but I should have recognized how much they look alike before this."

"Hey, I'm the detective. I'm the one who didn't do my job. Any patient who has you as a nurse is very, very fortunate."

"I still feel terrible about it. She may never wake up."

"With you taking care of her, she'll be out jogging before summer."

"About all I can do now is pray."

"We all know how good you are at that," he said, hugging her against him and brushing his lips over her forehead.

Elena smiled for the first time that day. Cesar might be a long way from accepting the Lord, but he made her happy by understanding that sometimes she had to give time to others.

Chapter Twenty-One

"Good news," James said as he met Elena on her way into the hospital Friday morning. "I have our flu patients."

"Maybe I'm not awake yet," she said, shaking her head. "What flu patients?"

He laughed at her confusion. "Nearly two hundred senior citizens have volunteered to act as the patients overwhelming our facilities Monday when we have the drill. We won't have to pretend to be swamped. We really will be."

"Oh my, that *is* realism."

"We have Candace's mother to thank. Janet spent hours and hours networking on the phone to find that many. The police are on board for extra security, and we have retired nurses and doctors to help out. The hospital board approved free lunches in the cafeteria for everyone who participates."

"My biggest worry is taking care of the patients we have. Won't all the extra activity interfere?"

"Hopefully, no. As long as we keep everyone informed, I don't think it will be a problem. Casual visitors will be denied entrance for a few hours, but that won't apply to the close relatives of ICU patients. The newspaper is giving us front-page coverage so the whole town should know what's going on."

"Have you heard the news about our coma patient?" she asked.

"Did she wake up?"

"No, but she's not a Jane Doe anymore. She's Maxine Newman's sister, if you can believe it. She was house-sitting when she fell. That's why no one reported her missing."

"Poor Maxine," James said, crinkling his brow in sympathy. "Speaking of the missing, the pet detective is coming to Deerford today to do some hands-on hunting for Sapphire. She thinks she can find her, but I'm not so sure. It's been a long time."

"For Fern's sake, I hope she's right."

Maxine was in the room with her sister when Elena reported for work. She felt a little weepy seeing the love and concern on her face, but she still had faith that the coma patient would return to consciousness someday.

"I have a million things to do before the drill," Maxine said. "Please promise that you'll call me if there's the slightest change."

"You don't need to ask," Elena assured her.

The world seemed a brighter place when Elena left the hospital after work. The rainy spell had finally passed and unseasonably warm weather reminded her of childhood pleasures: finding twigs and weaving them into little baskets, searching for pretty stones, seeing how high she could swing on the school playground.

It was a privilege and a pleasure to watch her granddaughter grow, but it was also a reminder of her own innocence as a child. She'd always been close to her mother, and it was one of the joys of her life that she'd located her restaurant in Deerford.

Izzy had been denied the early bonding years with her mother. How was it going to affect her in the future? Could Sarah make up for lost years and play an important role in her life?

Elena had many questions, but no answers.

Rafael worked the breakfast and lunch shifts at the restaurant, so he was available to pick up his daughter after school. Today they got home before Elena, and she could hear Izzy laughing as soon as she stepped into the house.

"Buela!" she cried out. "We're going to the park tomorrow."

"Only if the weather stays this nice," Rafael cautioned. "The weatherman says it will, but he can be wrong."

"Will you come too, Buela?" Izzy asked. "I want to feed the ducks."

"If they're there," her father warned.

Elena was pretty sure there would be plenty of wild ducks to feed. Many of them wintered in Deerford because a portion of the pond never froze, thanks to water that rushed in from upstream.

"I'll see if we have some stale bread for them," she said.

"They'll eat fresh bread too," Izzy seriously informed her. "Can my mama come?"

"If she isn't busy. You can call her."

"What do you want to do besides feeding the ducks?" she asked her granddaughter.

"Swing," Izzy said. "I want to go as high as the sky."

Elena smiled. She remembered feeling the same way when her biggest worry in life was avoiding the bully who liked to pull her hair on the playground. It saddened her that Izzy's big concern was getting her mother to come along. It comforted Elena that the two parents were starting to work together for their daughter's benefit.

The pet detective's van was parked in front of the house when James got home from work. He wasn't pleased that Mimi Zonn was inside talking to Fern. He'd hoped to avoid getting her hopes up, but he had to admit that sometimes he underestimated his wife.

She'd made tea in the kitchen and was chatting with the detective at the table in the breakfast nook as though they were old friends.

"Mimi has a new idea about finding Sapphire," Fern told him.

"Let's just keep it between you and me," the statuesque woman said in a confidential tone. "Don't want your hubby to be disappointed if my idea doesn't work out."

She was wearing a brown suede jacket that looked as if it had about fifty years wear on it. Her jeans were flannel lined, if the faded green plaid cuffs were any indication; and she'd pulled her hair back under a greasy baseball cap with a Milwaukee Braves logo, a franchise that had migrated south to Atlanta years ago.

James wanted to say that she could refund the big fee he'd paid if she didn't want him to be disappointed, but he refrained. It was worth the money to see the happy expression on Fern's face. Apparently she had more faith in the pet detective than he did.

Mimi wrapped half a dozen chocolate chip cookies in a paper napkin and stuck them in her jacket pocket.

"In case I get hungry," she said. "Solving this case may take a while."

Fern graciously walked to the front door with her, using her cane instead of the walker she used on days when her MS was particularly troubling.

"She has a very positive attitude," Fern said after closing the door. "After talking to her, I tend to believe she'll find Sapphire."

"Sapphire's been gone a long time," James said, worried that his wife's optimism would only lead to more disappointment.

"Dear, don't look so grim," she said. "I have a very good feeling about your pet detective."

"I'll be right back," he said, quickly going out the door in the hope of catching up with Mimi.

Her van was still there, but he didn't see her anywhere. Where could she have gone in such a short time? He went around to the backyard on the chance that she was looking at the place where Sapphire had last been seen. Maybe that was something that only helped detectives on television crime dramas because she certainly wasn't investigating in his yard.

He was about to go inside when he caught a glimpse of her in a neighbor's backyard two houses down. She was moving fast and, he thought, furtively. If she expected to find Sapphire wandering around so close to home, she was a worse detective than he believed her to be.

"What is she doing?" Fern asked when he went back inside.

"Going through the neighbors' backyards. I hope she's good with dogs. I wouldn't want to surprise the Doberman down on the corner."

"I wonder why she's doing that," Fern mused. "Oh well, it's her business. I expect she knows what she's doing."

James wasn't at all convinced of that, but at least if Mimi failed, Fern might give up on ever finding Sapphire. He liked the idea of getting a kitten for her. This would be a good time, while the boys were still at home to help her with it.

"I was so interested in talking to our pet detective that I almost forgot our good news. The house passed inspection, and the sale is going to go through. We should be able to close on it in a week or so."

"That *is* good news. It will be great to be a one-house family again."

After dinner, Gideon and Nelson both had plans of their own. James was glad they wouldn't be there when the pet detective returned. Fern was going to be terribly disappointed when she returned empty-handed. He would have to comfort her, and he didn't want the boys to give her any false hope. If Mimi didn't find their pet—and he was almost certain she wouldn't—he would have the hard job of convincing her that Sapphire would never be found.

As it happened, the boys came home and went to their rooms, and there was still no sign of the pet detective. Her van was still parked in front of their house, making him wonder whether she'd been arrested as a trespasser for walking through people's yards at night.

Fern looked tired. Her eyes had dark shadows, and she'd given up all pretense of reading.

"Why don't you go to bed?" he suggested. "I'll wait up until I hear something from Ms. Zonn."

"I'm sure I couldn't get to sleep. I have a feeling that we're going to get good news."

James doubted that there would be any news at all. It had been a long day at work and a longer evening waiting for the pet detective to return. His eyes were drooping, and he was too sleepy to stay awake much longer. The best he could do was nap in his easy chair. Then he would be sure to hear Mimi if she actually came back to their house.

He dreaded seeing her van still parked on the street in the morning. She looked like a woman who could take care of herself in almost any situation, and Deerford wasn't the south side of Chicago. Still, he was uneasy. She'd been gone too long.

When Fern finally dropped off to sleep on the couch, he napped in his chair.

Suddenly he was wide awake and rushing to the door. He was sure the doorbell had penetrated his dreams, and he hurriedly switched on the porch light and opened the door.

He had to be dreaming, but he heard Fern's voice behind him. This was real.

Mimi was standing on the porch with her arms full of fur, familiar silvery gray and smoky black fur.

"You've found her!" Fern actually squealed with pleasure.

James stepped back so the pet detective could come in. She put the cat on the floor, and Sapphire strutted toward the kitchen, as much at home as if she'd never gone missing.

"How?" James was as close to dumbfounded as he'd ever been. "How on earth did you find her?"

"I found a cat lady about ten blocks away from here."

"A cat lady?" Fern sounded as puzzled as he felt.

"You folks wouldn't have a bite to eat, would you? I ran out of cookies hours ago."

James would have emptied the fridge and freezer to hear what she had to say, but it was Fern who offered sandwiches with some sliced turkey they had on hand.

"Splendid!" Mimi said, making herself at home in their kitchen.

"Tell us," Fern prompted while James made several sandwiches liberally covered with mayo.

"It came to me all of a sudden," the pet detective said, stringing out her story for maximum effect. "I've run into a few cat ladies in my time."

"Do you mean women who own a cat?" Fern asked.

"Not *a* cat. Hoards of cats. I'm talking about people who take in so many strays that they can't even keep track of them. My instinct told me there had to be a cat lady in your town."

"We put up fliers everywhere," James said. "Sapphire wasn't a stray. She's a pampered pet. Why would anyone think otherwise?"

"That's what stumped me for a long time. Don't think I haven't been on the case, even when I wasn't in town."

"Please, tell us," Fern said, watching with pleasure as Sapphire wandered the room getting reacquainted with her home.

James thought she was being overly mysterious, but she'd earned the right to tell the story her way.

"I walked backyards looking for cat doors. It got a little risky once I had to use my powerful flashlight. A couple of dogs got a bit testy, but if you're not afraid, they usually back off."

"But what did you expect to find?" James was getting impatient now.

"Cat doors."

"Cat doors?"

"Cat ladies usually have cat doors."

"We had one at our other house," Fern said.

"They're convenient with one cat, almost essential when you're living with dozens and dozens. I found a couple of red herrings."

"False leads," Fern said, leaning forward on her chair.

"Exactly, but finally I found what I was looking for—a cat lady."

"With a cat door?" James said, still not sure where this was going.

"Yes, but she wasn't an ordinary cat lady. Sweet as pie, but blind as a bat." Mimi bit into one of the sandwiches.

"A *blind* cat lady?" James wondered if he was still dreaming and then Sapphire brushed against his leg, and he had to believe what Mimi was saying.

"Apparently your kitty wandered that way and got confused and then went through the lady's cat door."

"She must have thought it was the cat door at our other house," Fern said.

"Or else she smelled other cats and was curious," James said.

"Well, this lady had no idea that she had someone's pet. In fact, about all she can see these days are shapes and movement, so she hardly noticed that she had one more cat. Sapphire has been fed like a queen, along with thirty or forty others. She apologized for causing you folks so much worry; but as I said, she didn't even know she had an extra guest."

Fern lifted Sapphire onto her lap. "I don't know how to thank you."

"Ordinarily I charge extra for night work, but since it took me so long to latch onto the solution, we'll just call it even. You wouldn't have more of those cookies, would you?"

"We have some brownies in the freezer. It will only take a minute to thaw them in the microwave," Fern said.

"Happens I like them frozen," the pet detective said.

"Perfect." Fern grinned widely.

"Thank you, Mimi," James said. "If I hear of other lost animals, I'll be sure to recommend you." He couldn't believe his own words as he stroked Sapphire's head.

Chapter Twenty-Two

ELENA WOKE UP BEFORE SIX, EVEN THOUGH Saturday was her day off. It took her a few moments to realize why. Rain was beating on the roof, a bad sign for an outing in the park.

"Why are you up?" Cesar mumbled as she stood at the window looking out through a watery pane.

"It's raining."

"Come back to bed. There's nothing you can do to stop it."

"I'm just disappointed for Izzy's sake. She was really looking forward to the park."

"It will still be there tomorrow."

"That's not the point."

"My mother always said: 'rain before seven, clear before eleven.'"

"She also said that toads cause warts, and you should never put off until tomorrow what you can do today."

"*Um*, I think a fellow named Ben Franklin said that second thing."

"Whatever," Elena said, slipping back into bed. "Izzy really wants to feed the ducks. Rafael is going to bring home a big bag of stale tortillas from the restaurant."

"If they're stale already, they will keep another day."

"Maybe I'll pack a picnic lunch."

"It's raining," he said with a groan.

"Rain before seven—"

He rolled over and pulled the pillow over his head.

The rain turned to a gentle drizzle by nine o'clock, and by eleven it had stopped completely. A weak sun came out, and Izzy was totally convinced that everything would dry out by the time her father got home from working the breakfast shift.

When Elena warned her that the ground would still be wet, she got out her bright yellow boots and wore them around the house.

By noon she was glad she hadn't mentioned a picnic to her granddaughter. Although the sun was stronger, it was still winter coat weather. The log picnic tables in the park would be too damp, but fortunately Izzy wanted to feed ducks, not herself.

As expected, Cesar begged off going with them.

"Spring is nearly here," he said. "I have to take the lawn mower in for servicing and do a dozen other things."

"And watch the basketball game," Elena hissed at him when Izzy was out of hearing.

He grinned. "A man's gotta do what—"

"No, no! Enough with the sayings." She grinned back, glad her husband was in a good mood.

Izzy was so focused on ducks that she wouldn't miss her grandfather. The big question was whether Sarah would be joining them. Elena decided not to bring up the subject, not even when Rafael came home with a big sack of food for the ducks.

"I'll drive," he said as he handed the day-old tortillas to his daughter. "You'll have to tear them into smaller pieces. Ducks don't use knives and forks, you know."

Izzy thought that was hilarious, but Elena was a little on edge wondering whether Sarah was coming too.

She suggested that Rafael drive her car. It was smaller than his van, but there was still room for a fourth person. Neither Izzy nor her son mentioned Sarah, but he drove directly to the street where her apartment was. She was standing outside by the curb waiting for them.

"Mommy, look what I have to feed the ducks!" Izzy said when Sarah slid onto the backseat beside her. "I have to make little pieces so the ducks won't choke."

"Why don't we start tearing them up now?" Sarah suggested. "Then you'll be ready to feed the ducks."

After Rafael parked the car, the four of them walked down to the pond that was home to an ever-increasing flock of ducks. They were the only ones there, although Elena knew that people in town made regular visits to feed them through the winter.

All the ice had melted off the pond, but most of the ducks still congregated in the area that was their winter haven. Izzy hurried toward them, and that was all the invitation they needed. A noisy throng started swarming toward her, and Elena worried that the onslaught would overwhelm Izzy.

"Here, ducky," she cried out, quickly throwing bits of tortilla at the more aggressive ones.

One drake came up close, and for a moment Elena thought he would peck her granddaughter. Sarah quickly reached into the bag and tossed a piece directly at him, causing Izzy to laugh when he caught it in midair.

"They're really hungry!" she cried out. "Do you think we have enough for all of them, Daddy?"

"I have a small bag of bread crumbs in my purse," Sarah said, opening her big shoulder bag and taking it out.

"Why are some of them pretty and others not so pretty?" Izzy asked.

"The ones with shiny green heads are the boy ducks," Sarah said. "The plain brown ones are the girls."

"That's funny! Why are the boy ducks prettier than the girl ducks?" she asked.

Sarah and Rafael exchanged a look and both laughed.

"The boys look good so the girls will like them," Rafael explained.

"Then why didn't you wear your new green jacket so Mommy will like you?" Izzy asked.

"That's only for playing with the band," he said.

"You should wear it," Izzy insisted.

Both parents laughed, and Elena was happy that they could be together without the high level of stress or resentment that often clouded their relationship. Perhaps they were past all that tension.

She'd stopped expecting them to become a couple again, but for now she was proud of the way they were working together for their daughter's benefit.

Izzy developed a strategy for feeding the overly eager ducks without any prompting from her parents. She threw the food far enough to keep them from rushing at her.

After throwing the last morsel of food at a drake that was probably too well fed for his own good, she retrieved her mittens from her father's pocket and started backing away from the aggressive birds.

"Can I swing now?"

"I don't know why not," Rafael said, looking at Sarah for confirmation, a gesture that pleased Elena.

She hung back and watched as the three of them raced down the path to the play equipment. She'd taken Izzy there many times, sometimes with Rafael or Cesar, but this was a special outing for her granddaughter because both parents were with her.

Just as she started to follow them, she heard a familiar ringing. It was the cell phone in her purse, and she dug down to the bottom to answer before it stopped.

"You got a call from the hospital," Cesar said. "It sounded important, so I'm coming to pick you up and take you there. Where are you now?"

"Just leaving the duck pond to go watch Izzy swing. Do you know what's up?"

"No, only that you're wanted in ICU whenever you can get there. Watch for me."

She hurried over to the play area where Rafael was pushing Izzy on a swing and Sarah was cheering them on.

"I just got a call from your father," Elena said. "He's coming to pick me up. There must be some emergency at the hospital. They want me to come in."

"I could take you," Rafael quickly offered.

"No, he's on the way. Izzy's having too much fun to leave yet."

"I hope everything turns out okay," Sarah said with concern.

"So do I." She immediately thought of the specter of flu hanging over the hospital. It was so unusual for her to be called on her day off that this must be something serious, a major accident or disaster. Her heart pounded with anxiety, and she was glad Cesar was on the way.

Izzy waved good-bye from her perch on the swing, her legs pumping to go higher.

"Have fun, guys," she said, turning to go to the roadway to watch for Cesar.

"We will," Rafael said.

Was it possible all three of them were really enjoying being together? What did that mean for their relationship?

Cesar came almost as soon as she reached the road again. He didn't know any more than what he'd told her on the phone, but he drove her to the hospital in the shortest possible time.

"What do you want me to do?" he asked. "Come in with you? Wait until you know what's up?"

"I have no idea why I'm here or how long I'll be. Why don't you go home, and I'll call you when I know more."

Everything seemed calm on the main floor of the hospital, and she was the only one in the elevator as she went up to ICU. She expected to see the waiting lounge filled with anxious relatives and friends, but instead a lone woman sat reading a magazine. She was a familiar face as she'd been coming every day for the last week to see her elderly mother who was in critical condition.

She walked up to the nurses' station, expecting to hear why she'd been called, but the nurse supervisor on duty only told her to go to room 11.

The number immediately registered as Maxine's sister Jeanette's room. She practically ran, stopping in the open doorway in astonishment.

"I knew you'd want to know," Maxine said, rising from the chair that she'd pushed up to her sister's bedside.

"We can't thank you enough." The voice was weak, but there was no mistaking that it came from her coma patient.

"You're awake!"

"I can't believe that I was out for over two weeks," Jeanette said.

Maxine held her sister's hand and spoke softly. "This is my sister Jeanette. I told her how you connected us because we still look a lot alike."

"When did it happen?" It was all Elena could say.

"A little over two hours ago. We've had quite a parade of doctors here since then. Dr. Hamilton came right over. He was almost as excited as I am."

"He cares a great deal about his patients," Elena said.

"I hope I didn't interrupt anything important," Maxine said. "I wanted to share our happiness with you."

"No, I'm grateful that you did. It's so wonderful."

"I don't know how to thank you," Maxine said.

"Seeing the two of you together, able to talk—" Emotion choked off her words, and she silently offered a prayer of thanks. They talked quietly for a few minutes and then Elena thought it was best that she leave.

"I'm so happy for you, Jeanette. And you too, Maxine."

Riding down on the elevator, she was grateful for the happy ending to the sisters' story. Had Maxine's presence played a part in Jeanette's recovery? There was no way to know, but she liked to think that love had healing power.

Today was the most hopeful she'd felt in a long time. Her heart was singing to see the sisters truly reunited, but she was also grateful that the Lord had given Izzy a happy time with both her parents.

Chapter Twenty-Three

JAMES GOT TO THE HOSPITAL HALF AN HOUR EARLY Monday morning, but he didn't go to his usual workstation. Instead he went to the registration desk on the main floor that would serve as a command center for the preparedness drill. Albert Varner, Hope Haven's CEO, had been more than cooperative in letting the task force use the facilities as they wished. His support had been key in getting everything lined up, and he'd volunteered his executive assistant Penny Risser as a liaison between the administration and the medical staff. James wasn't quite sure how to use her, but no doubt she'd make herself useful in some capacity.

His only responsibility today was the drill. A substitute was covering for him in Med/Surg, although only emergency procedures were scheduled. Even though this was far different from his Gulf War drills, he felt a familiar surge of adrenaline. They were only practicing for an epidemic, but what they learned today might be helpful in any kind of disaster.

"Everything ready, James?" Dr. Weller asked, walking up to the desk. His hair was unruly, and a lab coat flapped around his calves, but there was a definite disconnect between his casual appearance and his energetic work habits.

The Emergency Room physician didn't look like a paragon of efficiency, but James had a lot of respect for his dedication. Most doctors were willing to help with the drill if it didn't interfere too much with their regular work, but Dr. Weller was giving it his all. The Emergency Room would be key in managing an epidemic, and James couldn't think of anyone he would rather have manning it.

"All we need are patients," James said.

"I hope our senior victims don't bring me too many real ailments along with mock flu symptoms," Dr. Weller joked. "We'll be swamped when the volunteer patients start coming."

"I heard the good news," Candace said while walking up to the two men. "Although I never thought I'd be happy to hear a new mother has pneumonia."

"Yes, your OB patient is out of isolation and will probably go home in a day or two," Dr. Weller said. "But we still have to take this drill very seriously. Three doctors in the county have reported seeing worrisome symptoms in young patients, all under the age of sixteen."

"That isn't what we expected to hear," James said with a frown, grateful that his boys had had the vaccine. "Not with the new strain of flu. By the way, your mother should get an award as volunteer of the year for lining up so many seniors to act as patients."

"She was happy to do it," Candace said. "As I understand it, half of the mock patients will crowd into Emergency, and the rest will come to the registration desk."

"Yes, hospital security and police volunteers will be outside throughout the drill to direct any real patients to the north entrance," James said. "Dr. Hamilton has set up a table outside the cafeteria to process them. Volunteers with wheelchairs will take them to the appropriate units."

"Everyone in the Birthing Unit understands that we'll be in virtual lockdown. No one leaves until we get the all clear," Candace said.

James rubbed his chin thoughtfully. "I think we have all bases covered. Remember, though, the drill will end in time for lunch to be sent up to the patients. In a real epidemic, we could be at this for days or even weeks."

Candace shuddered, and Dr. Weller looked grim.

"I hope people are driving carefully, and no school kids break their arms at recess. Fortunately, we have several other county hospitals on standby. Also we have a fleet of borrowed ambulances in case we have to evacuate anyone."

"Everything set?" Dr. Hamilton asked, walking up to them in a fresh white lab coat.

James smiled in spite of his responsibilities. Sometimes Dr. Hamilton reminded him of an old-fashioned country doctor in his heavily starched and meticulously ironed cotton coat, but looks were deceiving. The older doctor was as up-to-date on medical procedures as anyone in the hospital.

People scattered to take their posts for the drill; but James knew he had to remain at the hub, the registration desk, to handle any glitches in the plan.

"Good morning, James."

He turned to see Penny who, for some reason, was wearing a longish navy skirt and a white cotton shirt that made her look like a nineteenth-century nurse. She even had a plastic band stuck in her graying hair to add to the effect.

"Mr. Varner said I'm supposed to help here at the desk," she said.

He knew *help* and *take charge* were synonyms in her vocabulary and tried to think of something to keep her at bay.

"Maxine Newman is here already. You might want to check in with her in the community health office."

Maxine was the official head of the task force and the drill, although she was a dream administrator when it came to letting people do their jobs without throwing up roadblocks. She didn't really deserve having to deal with Penny, but James had faith that Maxine would find some harmless chore for her. It wasn't that Mr. Varner's executive assistant was inefficient. Just the opposite was true. She'd never met a problem that she couldn't solve with sheer force of will.

While he had a free moment, James made a quick call home to Fern. The boys were up, and Nelson was doing last-minute homework, which didn't particularly please his father. But he was much too busy to worry about it now. What would they find when they got to their schools? Would a lot of kids be out sick? Epidemics could hit any age group, but when flu was involved, it was usually the infirm and elderly who were the most vulnerable.

He hung up and was glad to see Elena walking toward him. She was working with Maxine on the communications part of the drill. He wondered what she'd heard about doctors diagnosing flu in young people. She looked unusually somber, not a good sign.

"What do you hear about flu hitting young people?" he asked without preamble.

"Four doctors have reported symptoms to the county health office," she said. "They all came through Emergency Rooms in other hospitals, but it's still too early in the morning to hear from doctors seeing patients in their offices."

"I heard three," he said with a worried expression.

"None have been confirmed."

"The state lab is so backed up, we could be in the middle of an epidemic before we know for sure."

"Maxine said they're bringing in extra help, maybe from the universities."

James heard the wail of an ambulance. Was it one of the borrowed units making an entrance, or were they bringing a real patient? He wanted to sprint to the Emergency Room, but his place was here. That was what drills were all about: everyone knowing what to do and doing it.

He thought of calling, but Dr. Weller and his staff had to handle whatever it was.

"Mrs. Newman doesn't have anything for me right now," Penny said, walking up to the desk and nodding a greeting to Elena.

"Good," James said. "You can go to the ER and see whether that ambulance brought us a real patient."

To her credit, she scurried off without questioning his instructions.

"I have to get to ICU," Elena said. "But I wish I could be down here. It will be agony wondering how the drill is going."

"And whether all the activity is part of the drill," James said to himself as she walked away.

He didn't have time to worry about that or anything else. Two Red Cross volunteers and the pastor of a local church came to the desk to help him, along with two off-duty nurses and the retired head of the Cardiac Unit. They all had a good handle on what they were supposed to do, and they didn't have to wait long until things got hectic.

The first of the mock patients came to the desk shortly after seven. She was a tall, stern-faced woman in her mid to late seventies, and she'd been well coached in her role.

"I'm so cold I can't stop shaking, and I'm afraid I'm going to pass out." She went through a list of complaints without leaving out any that suggested flu.

"Congratulations," James said. "You've remembered every symptom."

"I remembered them because they all happened to me," she said. "I was a young bride in 1957 when the Asian flu hit. I was so sick that my husband thought I'd die. I don't know how long I lay in bed, shaking like a leaf under every blanket we owned. I kept telling him that I was too sick to go to the doctor's office, but he finally made me—practically had to carry me. It was the first time they named the flu, as far as I can remember."

"I had that too," a pink-cheeked woman with fluffy white hair said as she stepped up to report her mock symptoms. "Never been that sick before or since. I was teaching school, my first year. More than half of the children in the seventh and eighth grades were absent and then the teachers started coming down with it too."

James was interested in their experiences, but more mock patients were coming into the hospital, and he had to keep things on track.

"Oh, I'm going to faint," a third woman said, clutching at the desk with one hand and her head with the other.

Two LPNs and several volunteers where standing by with wheelchairs, and he quickly motioned one of them to wheel the light-headed woman to the main-floor emergency station. She would be diagnosed and possibly sent to one of the cots in a section of the reception area curtained off for that purpose.

He couldn't help smiling as she was wheeled away moaning and groaning. The volunteer patients were really putting a lot into their roles. Maybe the town had more wannabe actors and actresses than anyone had suspected. He didn't have time to enjoy their performances, though. More pseudo patients were swarming into the hospital, and each one had to be interviewed quickly.

A few had been coached to present the wrong symptoms. One balding man with a deep tan that suggested he'd spent the winter in warmer climes tried to convince James that his aching shoulder was a flu symptom. It took some close questioning before he admitted that he only wanted some pain pills for the muscle ache he'd gotten playing golf.

The aides pushing wheelchairs had to run to keep up with the patients that James and the other nurses assigned to them.

"The Emergency Room is swamped," Penny said, rushing back to the registration desk. "Dr. Weller wants to know if you have any staff members or volunteers you can spare."

"Afraid not," James said. "We have more than we can handle."

He was in the middle of convincing an overly dramatic woman in her eighties that she should go see her regular physician for the pain in her knees.

"I'll take care of this," Penny said.

He didn't have time to pay attention to her, but, much to his surprise, Penny came back with the hospital CEO, the chaplain, and several lab workers.

A plump little lady was crying loudly, insisting that her husband must be dying because they'd wheeled him away. James turned the overly enthusiastic performer over to Penny and took two seconds to enjoy the sight of Mr. Varner pushing a wheelchair with a pseudopatient over to the cots.

The task force had been told to expect up to two hundred seniors to pose as patients. Apparently that group had told their friends and relatives, and the number of mock patients had mushroomed. The cots were all full, and makeshift mattresses spilled out beyond the curtained area. Finally James had to direct his helpers to send people directly to the cafeteria where all volunteers would have a nice buffet lunch. He sent Penny ahead to warn the kitchen staff to bring out anything they had to feed the increased numbers.

The preparedness drill ended at eleven o'clock, after four of the most hectic hours James had ever spent at Hope Haven.

The task force met in the conference room after it was over to assess the results. Mr. Varner ordered pizza brought in for lunch since the cafeteria staff had to use all the food they'd prepared to feed the large number of volunteers. He complimented everyone who'd participated, but James knew there were some serious flaws in their plan. They simply hadn't been prepared well enough for the huge numbers that came.

Dr. Hamilton had another point of view.

"It was the best possible drill," he said, "and I want to thank each and every one who participated, especially James Bell for all the work and thought he put into it."

James was uncomfortable with the accolade and protested.

"We needed more staff members and volunteers to handle the crowd. Also we didn't have enough cots or wheelchairs to accommodate all the potential patients."

"The same was true in the Emergency Room," Dr. Weller added.

"The point is, you handled it," Dr. Hamilton said. "You brought in more people, and every potential patient received attention. Not only that, the rest of the hospital continued to function smoothly."

"Thanks should also go to Penny Risser for finding more help," James said, giving credit where it was due.

"Yes, she demonstrated that an epidemic has to involve all hospital personnel, not just the medical staff. We learn from mistakes," Dr. Hamilton said. "When all the reports are done, we'll have an excellent picture of what we should and shouldn't do in a disaster situation. I'm especially pleased with the way Hope Haven worked with the county health department and Mrs. Newman. Is there anything you'd like to say, Maxine?"

"Only my sincere thanks for all you've done to make the drill a success."

When he was free for the day, James enjoyed remembering some of the seniors' performances. They ran from hysterical to hilarious, but one thing was certain. Everyone who participated took the drill seriously. That was all he could really ask for.

Chapter Twenty-Four

*I*DON'T KNOW WHY YOU BOUGHT THIS THING," Cameron said as he watched Anabelle remove a cuff from his arm at the kitchen table.

"For my peace of mind," she said, entering his blood pressure in a little booklet that came with the cuff and stethoscope. "I'm really happy with your reading this afternoon."

"It should be low," he said. "Babysitting with Lindsay Belle kept me hopping all morning. If I'd known how much fun a little grandchild is, I would've had one sooner."

She laughed and didn't say the obvious: They had no control over their children's interest in parenthood.

"I guess we'd better head into town for our lesson, although I don't know what salad dressing has to do with cooking. I was hoping we'd learn to make one of those fancy French dishes that nobody can pronounce," he complained.

"Not in the healthy cooking classes. If you'd ever read the labels on salad dressing bottles, you'd know how bad some are for you. They have high calories and high salt content, just the things you're supposed to avoid."

"Seems to me I'm supposed to avoid almost everything I like. Are you sure you want to go to class today?"

"We paid for it. We might as well go."

She used the one argument Cam would accept, but the truth was that she wasn't at all enthusiastic about going herself. She'd been cooking too many years to enjoy the beginners' approach Sherry used. She was capable of executing any recipe that struck her fancy, including ones that were good for her husband. But Cameron had enjoyed the tilapia lesson, although he'd made himself a little snack when they got home, claiming that he'd only had half a dinner.

His grumbling stopped as they drove into town, and she suspected that he liked the lessons more than he would admit.

At least they didn't have time for Cam to browse when they got to the Chef's Corner. Anabelle knew their kitchen had enough equipment to start a catering service, although much of it was old. Still, a kettle was a kettle, at least in her opinion.

"I'm just pleased as punch to see you all," Sherry said when her class members had lined up at their stations.

She was wearing a white shirt with blue butterflies and a cobalt blue skirt with three layers of ruffles at the bottom. The outfit made her look cute but no younger than she was.

Anabelle tied the apron that she'd washed and ironed, although she seemed to be the only one who'd bothered with an iron.

"I know some of you are disappointed that we're concentrating on salads today, but the terrible truth is that a plate of veggies can be higher in calories than a hamburger."

"I can't believe that," the young wife Hope said, snapping her gum.

"It's all in the dressing," Sherry said. "What we're going to make today is everyone's favorite Caesar salad."

"Is that the one with little black things in it?" Hope asked.

"Not everyone likes anchovies," the big man's wife said.

"Now I have to tell you right off that Caesar salad isn't a good choice for those who are trying to limit salt intake, but an anchovy is full of heart-healthy fish oils. For those of you who are concerned about sodium, I'll also show you how to make a lovely salad using my own recipe for a balsamic vinaigrette. Maybe you would like to try both."

"Will that be our whole dinner?" Cam asked, looking a bit appalled.

"You'll be surprised at how filling a good salad can be," Sherry assured him. "Now shall we get started? And don't fret yourselves about remembering the ingredients. I have printed copies for all of you to take home."

Much to her surprise, Anabelle enjoyed preparing the salad, although Cam seemed content to let her do most of the work. It was the first time she'd ever mashed an anchovy fillet, although she had experimented using paste that came in a tube. She'd never grated her own Parmesan cheese, but perhaps she would in the future now that she knew what a difference it made.

"Always dry your romaine or any other leafy greens thoroughly," their teacher said. "Today we'll just pat it dry with paper toweling, but I do stock a handy little gizmo that spin dries."

"I think we can do without one of those," Cam said, patting the romaine with something less than enthusiasm.

Anabelle counted the salad lesson as a success. Sherry had baked yeast rolls to go with it, and it seemed an adequate supper to her.

Cam admitted liking it but made himself some scrambled eggs when they got home.

"My blood pressure was fine today," he said as he smeared mayo across the eggs, his favorite way of embellishing them.

Anabelle shook her head but smiled at the man she loved. What they needed was a lifestyle change, not just cooking lessons. She would start working on that tomorrow.

"Why does Brooke get two birthdays?" Howie asked as he watched Candace light the thirteen candles on the chocolate cake his grandmother had made earlier in the day.

"I'm not getting two birthdays," his sister quickly protested. "This is my birthday, but when you get older, you don't have your party on a school night."

"Why not?" The glow of candles reflected in his eyes.

"Because my friends are too old for baby parties."

"I don't have baby parties," Howie protested.

"Let's sing 'Happy Birthday' so Brooke can blow out her candles," Candace said. "We don't want wax all over the frosting."

When the song and candle ritual were over, Brooke wanted to cut the cake herself.

"Why can't Mommy do it?" Howie asked. "Brooke will give me a tiny piece."

"It's my cake," Brooke said. "I want to cut it."

"Well, I want a big piece."

"Don't be such a piggy-pig," his sister taunted him.

"I'm not a piggy-pig!"

"Now children," Janet said in her soothing voice, "let's enjoy our cake. Who would like ice cream with it?"

"Me!" Howie said. "I want two scoops."

"None for me, thank you." Brooke put a large piece of cake on a plate for Howie and passed it to her grandmother. "I have to watch my weight. I don't want my new jeans to be tight."

Candace had decreed that all the girls wear jeans in case they decided to use any of the Y's athletic facilities. In fact, she didn't know what would entertain the mixed group. The girls, especially Brooke, would be disappointed if they did nothing but play basketball.

What games would interest kids that age? Candace had gone to the public library and checked out several books, but Brooke shot down all the suggestions she found in them.

At least her daughter approved of her selection of paper plates and napkins. She'd begged her not to buy anything with balloons or fuzzy animals, and Candace had settled on a restrained design with geometric shapes. They didn't say birthday to her, but Brooke was satisfied.

Brooke put a thin slice of cake on her own plate and took a dainty bite. When had her daughter gotten too old to enjoy her own birthday cake?

"Can I have another piece?" Howie asked, his mouth sticky from his first serving.

"Not right now," Candace said. "I don't want you to get a tummy ache."

"I won't. Just a tiny piece."

"I don't want you eating my whole cake," Brooke said. She put her fork down with half of her piece uneaten.

"You're not eating it. I bet Heath would let me have another piece."

It wasn't like her son to be so belligerent, not that he didn't squabble with his sister from time to time. This was something new, using Heath as a means of getting his way.

"No, he wouldn't," Brooke said. "It's my birthday cake, and he wouldn't want you to eat it all."

"Brooke! Howie! It doesn't matter what Heath would or wouldn't let you do. I said you've had enough, Howie, because I don't want you to get sick. That's it."

"Can I be excused?" Brooke asked. "I want to call Tiffany."

"Don't talk too long," Candace said. "I seem to recall that you have homework."

"Mother, it is my birthday. Maybe Howie is right. Heath is much more reasonable than you are."

Janet gave Candace a sympathetic look, but she made it a point never to interfere with her daughter's decisions about the children. For a few moments, she wished her mother would tell her how to handle a teenaged Brooke.

Was Heath more reasonable? Or would he agree to anything the children asked because he wanted them to like him?

After the kids had settled down for the night, Janet went to her room to read. Candace was tired, but she decided to hem a pair of new pants that were too long for Howie. As she stitched, she idly wondered how tall he would be as a man. Would he be lean and lanky like his father, or would his love of sweets make him chunky?

How would it affect him, not having his father to help him navigate growing up?

She couldn't help but think about Heath. They had fallen in love, and she believed he wanted to be part of her life for good. That meant being a father figure to her children, but she didn't know whether she was ready for that. What if his ideas about raising children were totally different from hers? They already looked to him to reverse decisions she had made.

The worst thing that could happen would be to make him part of their family and then lose him. How could Brooke possibly cope with losing both a father and a stepfather? If Heath did want to take their relationship to the next step, as she suspected he did, would it be in her children's best interests? Death or separation were frightening possibilities, and either would devastate Brooke. It might be even worse for Howie to have a stepfather for a short while and then lose him. He only had vague memories of his father, reinforced by the memory books, photographs, and Candace's stories about him; but he was already getting attached to Heath. Her son was so vulnerable. Both her children were.

She just didn't know whether to risk her children's happiness by taking a chance on Heath.

She put aside the sewing box and returned the needle to her pincushion. Howie didn't need his new pants tomorrow, and she didn't feel like finishing them tonight.

Before she could go upstairs to bed, the landline phone in the kitchen rang. She was tempted to let the answering machine get it, but she still had disasters on her mind after Monday's preparedness drill.

"Hello?"

"Hi." It was Heath. It was a sign of how close they'd become that she immediately recognized his voice. She smiled, glad to hear from him despite her prevailing fears.

"I'm not interrupting anything, am I?"

"Nope," she said, "I was just heading to bed."

"So early? You must have had a hard day."

"Yes, it's been a busy week so far."

"Well, get lots of rest so you don't get sick. I can't imagine chaperoning the girls and the boys at Brooke's party by myself."

"You won't have to." She suddenly realized that she didn't especially want him there. As much as she disliked the idea of boys at the party, she wanted Brooke to have a good time but play by her rules. She already knew that Heath was more lenient than she was. If two adults disagreed about what the children could and couldn't do, it would be a bad thing.

"I'm looking forward to it," he said.

"Heath, you really don't have to be there. It's never much fun to be a chaperone."

"Oh, I don't know. It's a chance for me to feel like a kid again. Play a little pin the tail on the donkey and musical chairs."

"I'm afraid Brooke and her friends have outgrown those games. We'll have some music, cake, that sort of thing."

"Sounds good. By the way, you can help me out. I'm not sure what to get Brooke."

"You don't need to get her a gift."

"I wouldn't think of showing up at the party empty-handed. One idea I have is a small TV for her room."

"That's much too big for a child's birthday gift."

"Do you think so? I wanted something special. After all, a girl only has a thirteenth birthday once."

"Heath, I really don't want her to have a television in her room."

"All right, no problem." She could hear the confusion in his voice. "Well, *uh* . . . can you give me any other ideas?"

"Sure," Candace said, trying to infuse some positivity into her tone. "You might consider a gift certificate for a small amount. Brooke loves clothes, but she's still happy with the merchandise at a superstore."

Her positivity may have been too late. Heath's tone was ever so slightly dejected. "I'll give it some thought."

After they hung up, Candace couldn't get Heath out of her mind. When the two of them were together, she loved his sense of humor and kindness. Not to mention his good looks. He was a good man, and she should be thankful that he cared for her.

She felt different when the four of them were together. Howie was eager to bond with him, and Brooke looked up to him as a father figure, but what if something happened to take him away from them? It would devastate them if Heath were taken from them as Dean had been.

Could she possibly take that risk? Would it mean putting her own happiness ahead of protecting her children?

She prayed for the wisdom to know what was right for her children.

Chapter Twenty-Five

WHEN SHE GOT HOME FROM RUNNING ERRANDS Saturday, Candace was nearly bowled over by Brooke's excitement.

Her grandmother had taken her to a beauty salon to have her hair done that morning. She looked older and more sophisticated with two blonde curls framing her face and the rest pulled back and anchored with a blue enameled hair clip. Even though there were hours to go before the party started, she'd changed into her new jeans and a gauzy white tunic with blue ribbons at the neckline and wrists.

"Why can't I go to the party?" Howie asked, appealing to his mother as soon as she stepped into the house.

"You're too young!" Brooke snapped, sounding as though she'd already told him that many times.

"Am not!"

"Howie," Candace said sympathetically, "you probably wouldn't have any fun. There won't be anyone there your age."

"I could play with Heath."

"Not this time," Candace said. "This is Brooke's party. When it's your birthday, you can have your own party."

"That's not for *ages*," he whined.

"We'll have a party just for the two of us," Janet said, coming into the hallway and taking his hand. "I thought maybe we could make popcorn and watch one of your movies. Or we could play board games. You're getting pretty good at checkers."

Candace smiled thanks at her mother and complimented Brooke on how pretty she looked.

"Wouldn't you like to change out of your tunic until it's time to go?"

She could envision a tragedy if she got a spot on it before the party.

"It's not as if I'll be able to eat a bite of dinner," Brooke said.

After that token protest, she went to her room to put on an old T-shirt. Sometimes mother still knew best.

Candace was almost as eager as Brooke when it was time to leave for the Y, only she was anxious to have it over. Maybe the children would all behave like angels, and everyone would have a wonderful time. At least she tried to convince herself that all would go well in spite of her misgivings.

Heath got to the party room before them and was already setting places at the long table.

"Here's the birthday girl and her beautiful mother!" he called out, sounding as excited as Brooke.

They didn't have time to talk. Guests started coming, even though the party didn't officially start for another fifteen minutes. So many came at once that it felt like a stampede, but Candace noticed that the girls were the early arrivals. Would the boys even show up? She didn't want to think about how hurt Brooke would be if none came.

She worried for nothing. Some were ten or fifteen minutes late, but by her count, every boy who had been invited showed up.

Except for a little rowdiness when two boys tried to get the same seat, the early part of the evening went better than Candace had expected. Maybe the girls weren't happy when the boys all clustered together at one end of the table, but everyone enjoyed the pizza and the four huge decorated cookies that Brooke had chosen instead of a regular cake.

Things started going downhill when several girls wanted to dance to the music piped in through the Y's sound system. A few of them danced with each other, but the boys certainly didn't take the hint and join them. In fact, several playful scuffles broke out, and Heath led them out to the gym for a game of basketball. The girls drifted out too, although they didn't look enthusiastic.

Candace followed, leaving the cleanup until later. No doubt the kids would be thirsty after the game, and maybe they would finish off the last of the birthday cookies.

Somehow Heath had gotten them to chose up teams, although a couple of the girls, Brooke included, lingered on the sidelines. He attempted to referee, but the game was more a free-for-all than organized basketball.

Suddenly Tiffany ran from the gym, and Candace followed after her. When she caught up, Brooke's friend had been sick in the rest room.

She was standing beside a sink softly crying, her face drained of color. A moment later Brooke rushed into the room, looking almost as devastated as Tiffany.

"Get my cell phone from my purse and call Tiffany's mother," Candace calmly directed her daughter.

"I never get sick. Why did I have to get sick tonight?" Tiffany wailed.

Candace did her best to comfort her, patting her face with moist paper towels and assuring her that there was no shame in getting sick. Even as she tended to the child, her thoughts went back to the preparedness drill and the task force. The symptoms that concerned everyone didn't include stomach problems, but she couldn't help but remember that children under eighteen were coming down with flu all over the county.

Tiffany's skin wasn't feverish to the touch, but the party was definitely over for her. Brooke stayed by her side until her mother came to take her home, gathering her things from the party room and walking to the car with them. Candace was proud of the way her daughter had cared for her friend instead of staying with the partygoers in the gym.

When the two of them went back to the game in progress, they both stood in shocked silence. Basketball had deteriorated into a rough game of dodge ball, and girls were shrieking in protest. One girl was hit hard between the shoulders and ran toward Candace for sanctuary.

Heath was in the midst of the confusion and finally managed to secure the ball, calling a halt to the activities. When he tried to get the basketball going again, it was no-go. A wrestling match broke out between two boys, and Candace found it was all the two of them could do to separate the two antagonists and keep the others from joining in. They ushered the sweaty, red-faced boys back to the party room, and the others followed.

Once everyone had settled down, Candace tried to rescue the party for Brooke's sake. She'd prepared several party games with prizes, but no one competed with any enthusiasm. She couldn't have been more relieved when parents started coming to pick up their children.

Heath helped clean up, but he was unusually quiet. He walked the two of them to Candace's car and opened the door for Brooke.

"I'm sorry that didn't go better," he said to Candace after closing the passenger-side door.

"It wasn't your fault." Candace tried to absolve him of blame, but she desperately wished she hadn't been persuaded to have boys at the party.

"I guess I've been away from kids that age too long."

She didn't have an answer for that.

"I'm driving to Peoria tomorrow," he said. "Would you like to come with me? I have to shop for boots before I go bird watching this spring, but we could do anything you like afterward."

"No, I don't think so." She apologized for refusing, but was she being honest with him?

"How about brunch? We could go right after church. Bring the whole family if you like."

She needed to talk to him but not at a family gathering.

"I'll meet you after church, just the two of us," she said, not sure why it seemed so urgent to talk to him.

"It was an awful party," Brooke said when Candace got into the car. "I wish I hadn't had a party at all."

"I'm sorry. No one can predict how other people will act. Maybe the boys just aren't mature enough for mixed parties."

"You didn't want me to invite them." Brooke stopped short of telling her she'd been right, but it was implicit in her silence.

Her daughter sounded so miserable that Candace wanted to cradle her like a baby, but that wouldn't make her feel better.

"Maybe I should have planned it differently," she said, trying to soothe away some of Brooke's misery. "Next year we'll think of a better way to celebrate your birthday."

"I never want another party, ever! I don't even want to go to someone else's."

Candace knew her daughter would change her mind and go to Tiffany's party, but this wasn't the time to say so.

"There are other kinds of parties," she said. "Maybe roller skating or bowling."

"Oh, Mother, only little kids have bowling parties."

"Well, we don't need to talk about it now. Some parts of your party were very nice. I'm sorry Tiffany got sick, though. She must feel terrible about it."

"At least I didn't throw up."

It wasn't much to be grateful for, but Candace was glad for anything positive Brooke had to say.

When they got home, Brooke mumbled good night to her grandmother and went to bed without any urging.

Candace had a restless night, but it wasn't just because Brooke was terribly distressed about the ruined party. In just a little over a year, Candace would be forty; and she didn't have a clear idea of where her life was going.

Was it right to let Heath take Dean's place in her children's affections? He was a well-meaning man, in spite of the fiasco at the party. That was her fault, really, for giving in against her better judgment.

At dawn she awoke feeling as though she'd tossed and turned all night. She prayed for the wisdom to make the right decision, but in the end, the children were her greatest responsibility.

Brooke didn't blame Heath for talking her mother into having boys at the party, but she was terribly let down. She'd expected something entirely different, but nothing worked out right.

Her daughter would recover from her disappointment, although the party certainly would remain a bad memory. But what would happen if Brooke came to love Heath as a stepfather, and he was taken from them as Dean had been? Could she risk her children losing a second father figure?

The question plagued her as she got Howie ready for Sunday school. Brooke begged off, saying that she had a headache. Ordinarily Candace would have been skeptical, but she understood her daughter's reluctance to face friends at church right after the disastrous party. She let compassion be her guide and allowed Brooke to stay in bed.

Candace sat through the church service in a haze, knowing what she should do but still not sure it was the right thing. She didn't make a firm decision until she pulled into the parking lot of the restaurant where she was meeting Heath.

She didn't see his Jeep, so she waited in her Honda CRV until he pulled up and then hurried over to head him off.

"Good morning," he said in a cheerful voice that only made what she had to do harder.

"I'm really not hungry," she said. "Could we just talk for a few minutes?"

"Is something wrong? Is everyone all right at home?" His concern made it even harder to do what she had to do.

"Can we sit in your Jeep for a few minutes?"

"Of course." He took her arm and guided her, opening the door for her and going around to the other side to take his place beside her.

"Heath, I don't know how to say this."

"We've always been up front with each other. Tell me if something's wrong. Are you upset about the party? I see now that I was wrong to encourage you to let Brooke invite boys. I guess I'd forgotten how adolescents behave."

"No, it's not that."

"What then?" His sympathetic tone made it even more difficult to say what had to be said.

"Brooke had a terrible time after her father died."

"Yes, you told me. She didn't speak for two months afterward. I realize how fragile she is."

"I'm afraid, Heath."

He reached over and took her hand, but she pulled it away. "Tell me."

"Not for myself. For my children. I can't let them be devastated again. They're becoming attached to you. If something happened to take you away from them, I don't know how they would cope."

"I'm not going anywhere," he said in a low voice.

"Not willingly perhaps."

"I understand. You're afraid to take a chance on us. If something happened..."

He did understand. That was the hardest part. He'd lost his fiancée, someone he deeply loved. He'd experienced the agony of loss and knew why she was so reluctant to take a chance on a future together.

"This isn't what I want." Tears were streaming down her cheeks in spite of her effort to hold them back.

He reached over and touched her face, brushing aside an errant tear.

"Me either."

"If my children weren't so vulnerable—every time you got into a car or went out into the wilderness to look for birds..." It was no use. She couldn't fully explain her fear.

They sat in silence for a few moments.

"Does this mean we won't see each other anymore?"

She'd never heard him sound so sad.

"For now." It wasn't a satisfactory answer, but it was the best she could do.

"Tell Brooke and Howie that I think they're wonderful young people."

"I will."

"I love you Candace. No matter what."

Tears pooled once again. "I love you too, Heath."

She quietly opened the door and got out and then walked across to her own car without a backward glance. Her vision was blurred by tears, and it took several minutes before she trusted herself to drive. By then, Heath's Jeep was gone.

As much as it hurt, she had made sure her children wouldn't have their lives devastated again.

And it did hurt.

Chapter Twenty-Six

CAMERON KEPT ANABELLE TOTALLY IN THE DARK. HE even insisted that she stay on after church for a brief worship committee meeting, although she could easily have gotten out of it on the excuse that they were having company.

It had been her husband's idea to invite Dr. Hamilton for Sunday brunch, a meal that he was preparing totally on his own. His wife, Anabelle's good friend and quilting partner Genna, was out of town for two weeks visiting relatives in the Chicago area. The doctor had been very happy to accept their invitation.

The big question was: What was Cam up to? They'd only had a couple of cooking lessons, and he'd been unimpressed by the salad recipes. Was he using their guest as an excuse to prepare a high-calorie meal, or did he have something else up his sleeve?

The doctor's car was in the drive when she got home, and the two men were in the kitchen engrossed in conversation. They went silent when she walked into the room.

After exchanging greetings, Anabelle looked around the kitchen with interest. Whatever Cam was preparing was in the oven, and he'd spirited away any cooking utensils. He hadn't left a clue, even covering a plate with a linen towel.

"Nice of you to have me over," Dr. Hamilton said. "I try to avoid my own cooking as much as possible."

"Cam has taken a real interest in it," Anabelle proudly told him. "We're even taking cooking lessons together."

"I'm especially glad to be here today," he said. "I have news about the flu."

"No more cases?" she asked optimistically.

"Afraid not. Over the weekend there've been thirty-two new cases reported countywide, but they've all been in young people under the age of seventeen. This is the bad news, but there is a positive side."

"It narrows the age range of potential victims," Anabelle said, anticipating what he had to say.

"Exactly. We only need to target the most vulnerable group, the children. Many of them have already had shots, thanks to early cooperation from the schools and the county health agency. We're going to have enough vaccine to inoculate every young person who comes to us, and we've been promised that the shortage will be over by the end of the month. Maxine is sending out e-mails urging physicians in the area to contact the eligible ones on their patient lists. I'm cautiously optimistic that we can lick this strain, at least in the present."

"That's wonderful!" Anabelle hadn't heard news this good in a long time.

"The task force did a fine job on the preparedness drill," he continued. "I have to thank you for all the volunteer time you put into it."

"It was well worth it, although I'm surprised that seniors, especially the elderly and infirm, don't seem to be coming down with it."

"No doubt there will be a lot of studies, but my opinion is that the Asian strain of flu that hit hard in 1957 and 1958 gave immunity to a lot of potential victims. I guess this is one time that we can be grateful for an epidemic, albeit one that hit over fifty years ago."

"Now if you folks are through talking shop," Cameron said, "you can take your places at the table."

Anabelle's curiosity grew as they waited for her husband to serve them. She swelled with pride when he put a long glass pan on the table and started serving up a lovely breakfast casserole.

"I used eggs, spinach, and mushrooms with a sprinkling of Parmesan," he said. "No salt, only a few secret seasonings that I may share with my wife. Or maybe not. I've taken to this cooking like a duck to water."

He had lovely fruit cups at each place and proudly produced a plate of bran muffins.

"Did you know that you can use stiff egg whites in place of shortening in some muffin recipes?" he said.

Not only was the brunch good for his blood pressure and heart, it was delicious. Anabelle enjoyed every bite, but she did have one question: Where was her real husband?

James spent the day Sunday feeling more relaxed and at peace than he had in weeks. It looked like Deerford would escape a full-blown flu epidemic, and his personal life had taken a turn for the better. The payment from the house sale was tucked away in the bank, and they could now decide whether or not to purchase the house they were renting.

Best of all, Fern was in good spirits and her MS wasn't troubling her nearly as much as it had been. James gave heartfelt thanks to the Lord in prayer again and again as he went through the day's activities.

Much to his surprise, Fern made two batches of her delicious cinnamon rolls for their brunch after church.

"What did we do to deserve a treat like this?" he asked, snagging a bit of frosting from the edge of one of the pans. "One for today, and one for tomorrow."

"Wrong," she said in a teasing tone. "The second pan is for the cat lady who took care of Sapphire. Even though she didn't notice the extra cat, she must have lavished attention on our runaway. She came home fat and sassy. I thought we could drop the rolls off later in the day."

"Good idea," James said, grateful for the thoughtfulness of his wife.

"Hey, what smells so good?" Nelson asked, bounding into the kitchen wearing a faded red shirt that could have come from the rag bag.

"Goodness, I thought you threw that shirt away ages ago," Fern said.

"I dressed up for church," he argued.

"Of course you did," James said with a grin. "I don't need to tell you how to dress anymore."

"While we're on the subject of clothing," Gideon said as he came into the room, "did you have to wear that ratty tweed sports coat this morning?"

James laughed in unison with Fern. When had their son changed from sloppy-boy mode to fashion consultant?

"Next week I'll wear my brown suit," James said in a good-natured voice.

"But don't wear that yellow tie with it," Nelson chimed in. "It doesn't look dignified."

Dignified! James smiled broadly, feeling extraordinarily blessed by his family, his career, and his faith.

Chapter Twenty-Seven

CANDACE WAS GLAD SHE'D HELPED OUT BY WORKING on Saturday even though she felt unusually drained of energy Monday morning. At least the worst of the flu threat had bypassed them, and she wasn't quite so worried about an epidemic in the Birthing Unit.

What really made her feel bad was the rift between Heath and her. A week had passed since she put the brakes on their relationship, and she missed his cheerful phone calls. Her house seemed empty Saturday evening without him to share a movie or a long talk.

Sunday was even worse. Both kids felt let down that he hadn't come to see them. Howie, especially, was disappointed because he wanted to challenge Heath in one of his board games. But Candace knew that she missed him far more than her children. His understanding and warmth made her feel young and vibrant again.

The morning dragged with only one new patient who probably wouldn't be ready to deliver until evening or later. Riley was involved in catching up on reports, and there wasn't much to distract Candace from her gloomy thoughts.

She didn't especially welcome her lunch break. It meant that she still had hours of relative inactivity before she could go home unless things got busy in the Birthing Unit.

Before she could pick up a tray to go through the cafeteria line, she felt a hand on her arm.

"Come to lunch with me," Heath said.

She didn't even think of saying no. "I'll get my coat."

"It's warmed up quite a bit. You can use my jacket."

He draped his dark green Windbreaker over her shoulders and hustled her out of the hospital.

"My Jeep is in the back," he said.

"We can walk to the Corner. It's a beautiful sunny day for this time of year," she said.

"Not before I say what I have to say." He took her hand and led her around the corner of the building, but they stopped before she could even see his vehicle.

"I spent the whole weekend thinking of what I could say to you," he said.

She wanted to say so many things to him that she didn't know where to start.

He didn't give her a chance. "I know I was out of line, trying to play super father to your kids. I adore them, but you're a wonderful mother. I never meant to interfere."

"You didn't interfere. The kids adore you. They missed you this weekend."

"I missed them, but my days were empty without seeing you." He pulled her closer to a windowless brick wall, shivering a little because the April wind was still chilly.

"Mine too." Candace felt tears of happiness welling up in her eyes.

"Don't cry. What I want more than anything in the world is for you to be happy." He brushed a tear away from her cheek and put his arms around her.

"Please, Candace, give me another chance. I love you more than I have words to tell you. I'm not trying to replace your husband or the children's father, but I think there's something important between us."

"I was afraid, Heath. I didn't know what I'd do if I let myself love you, if I let the children make you part of their lives, and then we lost you."

"There are no guarantees in life," he said so softly she just barely heard. "We take chances every day of our lives, but it's so much better to risk loss than not to have loved at all. I've thought and prayed about what our love would mean to us and the children, and I think our faith will see us through the rough spots."

Candace was silent for several long moments, but when she answered, her heart spoke for her.

"I'm blessed to have you in my life, and so are the children," she whispered.

Heath's arms closed around her, and she thanked the Lord for giving her this second chance at happiness.

Before Elena could get to the elevator, Penny rushed toward her waving a manila envelope.

"This came to the hospital for you," the executive assistant said, her cheeks unusually pink from rushing to catch up. "You really shouldn't have personal mail sent here."

"I don't know what it is," Elena said, "so how could I stop the mail carrier from bringing it here?"

"Well..." Penny said, apparently stumped for an answer. "Just so long as you don't make a habit of it."

Elena was alone when the elevator door closed, so she quickly opened the envelope and pulled out the large photograph and the enclosed note.

Dear Friend Elena,

I can't possibly thank you enough for completing my beautiful quinceañera gown. It is the most beautiful I've ever seen. I'm sure it helped my grandmamma recover more quickly from her surgery, knowing that you finished what she had begun.

God bless you for your great kindness.

Rosa Acuna

Elena stared at the photograph of a beautiful young girl with her dark hair pulled back from her forehead and held in place by a small veil. She had delicate features and a shy but pleased smile. The dress hugged a tiny waist and flowed to the ground, showing only the tips of her ballerina style shoes. She was wearing elbow-length white gloves and holding a bouquet of flowers, looking like a bride but too young to take such a serious step.

She couldn't help but compare her to Izzy. Someday her granddaughter would be a lovely teenager like the girl in the photograph, but Elena was grateful for every day of her childhood that she was allowed to share.

When she got to her unit, she put the envelope in a safe place behind the nurses' station. She would read the note again on her afternoon break, but for now, she was grateful for the boost it had given to her spirit.

Not surprisingly, Cesar had refused to go to the Sunday evening Bible study with her the last two weeks. She went alone, but it had been hard to concentrate. She missed being with him and regretted that he didn't share this important part of her life. At least they would go together to Izzy's recital this evening.

At supper time Izzy was too excited to do more than nibble at her food. Elena finally covered her plate with plastic wrap and put it in the fridge, anticipating that she could warm it in the microwave after the recital.

She helped her granddaughter get into the pretty little costume she'd made. The pink dye had worked well on her tights, and her tutu was suitably bouncy and cute.

"Can I put my shoes on now?" Izzy asked. "I want to see my costume all together."

"Best to wait. We don't have time to put them on and take them off before we leave."

She put them in Izzy's shoe bag before she could protest. Ballet shoes weren't meant for outside wear.

Rafael parked the car while Elena and Cesar went into the elementary school, rented for the occasion by Izzy's teacher. It was an older building, but it featured a nice stage at one end of the gym. Rafael took his daughter through the door that led to the backstage area while Elena and Cesar found four vacant folding chairs close to the front, saving the extra one for Sarah. They were early, thanks to Izzy's impatient urging, so the seats around them weren't occupied yet.

Cesar had been unusually quiet all through dinner and the ride to the school, but as soon as they were seated, he began talking in a low voice that only she could hear.

"I let you down, I know," he said.

"If you don't feel the love of the Lord in your heart, I wouldn't want you to pretend for my sake."

"I told you I would go to the class, but I felt like a hypocrite. I see things differently than the pastor. I didn't want to embarrass you by playing devil's advocate in front of the class."

"Pastor Flynn welcomes questions. You wouldn't embarrass me."

"Still, I'm sorry I can't share something so important to you."

She reached over and put her hand on top of his. "I pray every day that you'll come to know the Lord, but it's your decision. I won't try to force you to do anything at the church. It's meaningless if you only go to please me."

A couple edged past them to take the seats at the other end of the row; and a few moments later, Rafael and then Sarah came to sit in the chairs they'd saved for them.

Cesar took Elena's hand and held it until the first group of little ballerinas began their part of the program. There were seven children lined up on the stage when the teacher began playing the piano and nodding at them to begin.

Izzy's face was serious, and she executed her steps with concentrated precision. In fact, the little girl beside her kept looking at her, as though following Izzy's lead. Sitting beside Cesar, Rafael was recording every minute of the dance with his camera.

Elena allowed herself a moment of irony when the number was complete. It had lasted only minutes, compared to the hours it took to make the costume. But sewing for Izzy was a labor of love, and she really didn't regret the time it took.

When the older children had had their turns and the program was complete, Rafael and Sarah went backstage to collect their daughter. Elena went with Cesar to bring the car up to the door.

Big wet snowflakes blew into their faces and melted as soon as they hit the ground. Cesar took her arm as they weaved their way though parked cars to the place where he had parked.

"She did well," he said.

"Yes, I'm so proud of her."

"We have a great family."

"Yes."

"You're the heart of it. I can't imagine life without you," he said.

He pulled her close in the shadow of the car and lightly brushed her forehead with his lips.

"I'm sorry I'm not able to commit to the church. I want to make you happy, but I'm not ready. I hope it's enough that we share our family and our love for each other. Maybe someday..." His voice trailed off.

"We're blessed to have each other and Rafael and Izzy," Elena said, meaning it wholeheartedly.

"Yes. I love all of you more than I can say," her husband said.

Elena felt the peace of the Lord flowing into her. She trusted that someday her prayers would be answered and Cesar would believe as she did. Meanwhile, her heart was full of gratitude for all that they shared, especially their love for each other and their family.

About the Authors

Pam Hanson and Barbara Andrews are a daughter/mother writing team. They have had nearly thirty books published together, including several for Guideposts in the series Tales from Grace Chapel Inn.

Pam's background is in journalism, and she previously taught at the university level for fifteen years. She and her college professor husband have two sons. Reading is her favorite pastime, and she enjoys being a volunteer youth leader at her church. Pam writes about faith and family at http://pamshanson.blogspot.com.

Previous to their partnership, Barbara had twenty-one novels published under her own name. She began her career by writing Sunday school stories and contributing to antiques publications. Currently, she writes a column and articles about collectible postcards. For the past twenty-five years, Barbara has conducted sales of antique postcards to benefit world hunger relief. She is the mother of four and the grandmother of eight. Barbara makes her home with Pam and her family in Nebraska.

Read on for a sneak peek of the next exciting and heartfelt book in *Stories from Hope Haven*.

Lean on Me
by
Leslie Gould

JAMES BELL PUSHED THE ARM OF THE OVERHEAD light away from the operating table as Dr. Drew Hamilton stepped away from their sixty-eight-year-old patient. They'd just completed a stent placement.

"She'll be playing with her grandkids in no time." Dr. Hamilton's voice was muffled by his mask, and his eyes twinkled under his blue cap.

James nodded. There was nothing more rewarding than changing the course of a person's life.

"I'll wheel her down to recovery," James said as his pager went off. He squinted in the dim light to read the message. The CEO of Hope Haven Hospital, Albert Varner, wanted James to stop by.

Dr. Hamilton pulled his pager from the waistband of his scrubs at the same time. He glanced down, pushed a button, and then lifted his head toward James. "Albert Varner."

James's pulse quickened. "Does he want to see you too?"

Dr. Hamilton nodded. "I'll head down in a few minutes."

"What do you think he wants?" James gripped the end of the gurney.

"Probably to tell us what a great job we're doing." He patted James on the back. "See you soon."

James tried to smile but an uneasy feeling settled in his gut. The chief executive officer of Hope Haven wouldn't ask to see them to tell them that.

Twenty minutes later, after having delivered his patient to recovery, James headed down the staircase to the administrative offices. Penny Risser sat at her desk flanked by pots of two-feet-high plants, thick with leaves. Her lacquered fingernails clacked out a rhythm as she talked on the phone.

"What can I do for you?" Penny asked as she hung up the phone.

"Albert paged me."

"There you are." The CEO stepped forward, scanning the waiting area. "Where's Drew?" His dark hair needed to be combed, his tie was loose, and the sleeves of his white dress shirt were rolled to his elbows.

"He's on his way," James said.

"Come on in," Albert said.

James followed and passed through the door into a virtual jungle of plants, all thanks to Penny's green thumb. Bamboo grew in potted plants under the window. A hanging basket filled the far corner and three smaller plants—a fern, a zebra plant, and a tropical lily—graced the front of Albert's desk, partially hiding the mess of papers and files.

"James," Albert said, running his fingers through his thick hair as he sat down, "how are you doing?" The man was usually outgoing and gregarious although unorganized, but today he seemed more out of sorts than usual. He settled into his stately office chair behind the desk and rolled forward.

"Just fine, thank you," James said, though he felt ill at ease.

Just then Dr. Hamilton stepped through the doorway, saving James from having to say anything more. "Sorry to keep you waiting."

Albert stood and extended his hand, saying, "Drew. Welcome."

Dr. Hamilton shook it enthusiastically and then settled into the chair beside James. "I have to tell you, Albert," he said, "we've been busy all week and next week is already booked. Patients who would have gone to Peoria are now staying in town for their procedures. And the whole health of the town will improve with more consistent treatment and education."

Albert ran his fingers through his full head of hair again. "Actually Drew—and James—that's why I called you in. It turns out"—he cleared his throat—"that we may have made the decision to approve the Holistic Cardiac Program prematurely."

Dr. Hamilton scooted forward on his chair. "Say again?"

"You know," Albert said, pulling his chair closer to his desk. "Zane should really be here to explain the ins and outs of all of this." He picked up his phone and punched a couple of buttons. A couple of seconds later he said, "I need you in my office to spout some numbers." He glanced from James to Dr. Hamilton as he spoke but didn't smile. "On the Holistic Cardiac Program. Why it's not sustainable." Then he hung up the phone.

"He'll be right in," he said.

James's heart began to race.

"Albert," Dr. Hamilton said as he scooted to the edge of his chair, "we went over the numbers."

Before Dr. Hamilton could say any more, there was a quick rap on the door as it swung open, and Zane McGarry, chief financial officer of Hope Haven, strode into the office with a file in his hand. "Drew. James," he said, shaking both of their hands as the men stood. "Albert." He faced his boss and then sat in the chair closest to the door. He was an intelligent man, which was evident in his clear brown eyes. He sat tall and waited.

"Zane," Albert said, "I was saying that we're going to have to cut the new program." The CEO was usually charismatic, and James was surprised at his bluntness.

Zane nodded, a look of empathy on his face. "The timing is most unfortunate," he said. "We've just been notified of new national electronic-charting standards we need to meet and our budget can't weather both the new requirements and the new program."

"But how can Hope Haven survive if patients are going to Peoria for procedures and surgeries?" Dr. Hamilton said, leaning forward in his chair.

"At this point we're just trying to keep afloat and last as long as we can," Zane said.

Albert's head jerked forward. "Wait a minute, Zane. That's strictly your opinion." He shot a stern look at Zane. "And I've already told you, it's an opinion I don't share. I'm certain Hope

Haven will survive." He paused and then continued, "There's no reason to be pessimistic. We're closing one program—not an entire hospital."

"What's the timeline on the cardiac program?" Dr. Hamilton asked.

Albert shook his head. "There isn't one. We had to pull the plug, no pun intended, today. Right now."

"What about the patients who are scheduled for next week?"

"The regular surgery team will incorporate what they can—the others will have to go to Princeton or Peoria." Albert stood. "Drew, you'll go back to your previous position."

James stood. He'd be going back to the floor—and that would be fine. He would manage.

"And you, James." Albert's face reddened as he spoke. "According to human resources... I'm sorry James."

"Pardon? Sorry for what?"

"I'm sorry," Albert repeated. "You've been laid off."

"But..." He felt his stomach flip. "I've worked at Hope Haven for twenty-one years!"

Albert rubbed the back of his neck and turned his head toward Zane. "Do you remember exactly what human resources said?"

Zane stood. "I wasn't at that meeting."

Albert motioned to the door. "Zane, would you ask Penny to come in here for a moment?"

To James, it felt like an eternity before Penny joined them. She lingered at the doorway, barely entering the room.

Albert's face was beet red now. "Penny, what were the details on James's new job?"

Penny's face was full of compassion, but she sounded like a robot. "With the new position came a higher salary, but you gave up your seniority, and since your previous job has already been filled, the hospital regrettably has to lay you off."

James sat back down in his chair.

"It has nothing to do with your job performance—" Albert was saying as Dr. Hamilton interrupted him.

"This is outrageous!" The doctor's voice was loud and firm. "Hope Haven has never treated a loyal employee this way."

Zane appeared obviously distressed. Beads of sweat had gathered around the hairline of his closely cropped hair. "Albert, if you don't need me any longer, I have work to finish up." He slipped past Penny before Albert responded.

Albert sank down into his office chair. "This has nothing to do with you and James—it has to do with keeping Hope Haven open." He pushed back toward the window. "Even so, James, I have to ask you to gather all of your things, and you must also refrain from discussing this with any of the staff as you leave. I don't want a mutiny on my hands before I can address this in a civil way. That will happen Monday."

Dr. Hamilton shook his head. "If you think I'm not going to talk with anyone about this, you're mistaken. I'm not going to let this go," he said.

James headed to the third-floor staff lounge. He didn't have much to gather—just his coffee cup, an extra set of clothes in his locker, and his stethoscope, penlight, and clamps. He took the stairs to the first floor and then hustled down the hall by the ER and out the back door to the staff parking lot into the chill of the afternoon, hoping he wouldn't see anyone. But of course that wasn't possible.

"James!" Anabelle was standing beside her car. "How are you?"

His van was parked a couple of spaces away. He willed himself not to tell her what was going on. He never understood the power a company had over someone who had been laid off—until now. He wanted—he needed—to work at Hope Haven. He would comply with Albert Varner's instructions to a tee and hope Leila Hargrave could save the day come Monday.

"Good," James called out to his friend. "How are you?"

"Glad it's Friday," she answered. "What a week. You and Dr. Hamilton kept the floor hopping with all of your surgeries. I might have to hire some nurses just to keep up."

James grimaced at the irony of her statement.

Anabelle smiled. "What do you have planned for the weekend?"

"Oh, you know, the usual." *Praying.* "Catching up on laundry. Cleaning." *Updating my resumé.* "Playing basketball with Gideon and Nelson. Hanging out with Fern." Fern. His heart skipped a beat. "How about you?"

"I get to spend time with Lindsay Belle tomorrow." Anabelle beamed. The woman was crazy about her one-year-old granddaughter.

They said good-bye, and as James climbed into his van he thought about the layoff scare Hope Haven had experienced just over two years ago. Then, everyone was in the same boat. Now, he felt like a lone, isolated target. He took a deep breath and came to his senses. Thank goodness it was just him—hopefully Zane was wrong and there wouldn't be a ripple effect.

Frustrated, James pressed his forehead against the steering wheel. It had been less than two years ago that it looked like the hospital was going to close, and he'd considered moving his family to Peoria. And not long after that, the staff took a 10 percent pay cut to keep the hospital in the black. Surely Albert was right that the hospital wasn't facing such dire straits again.

James turned his eyes toward the hospital. The sun was low in the early spring sky, but it cast a shimmer of light over the bricks and windows. He turned on the ignition and let it idle for a minute before turning on the heater.

At least their previous home had sold last month. He'd begun the paperwork for a loan to buy their new place. If he really didn't have a job, he was pretty sure they wouldn't be approved for the house.

As he drove away from the hospital, he prayed aloud, "What now, Lord? What do You have planned for me, Fern, and our boys?"

To read *Lean on Me* in its entirety,
you can order by mail:
Guideposts
PO Box 5815
Harlan, Iowa 51593
by phone: (800) 932-2145
or online: shopguideposts.com

A Note from the Editors

Guideposts, a nonprofit organization, touches millions of lives every day through products and services that inspire, encourage, and uplift. Our magazines, books, prayer network, and outreach programs help people connect their faith-filled values to their daily lives.

Your purchase of *Stories from Hope Haven* does make a difference! To comfort hospitalized children, Guideposts Outreach has created Comfort Kits for free distribution. A hospital can be a very scary place for sick children. With all the hustle and bustle going on around them, the strange surroundings, and the pain they're experiencing, is it any wonder kids need a little relief?

Inside each easy-to-carry Comfort Kit is a prayer card, a journal, a pack of crayons, an "I'm Special" wristband to wear alongside the hospital-issued one, and a plush golden star pillow to cuddle. It's a welcome gift and has a powerful effect in helping to soothe a child's fears.

To learn more about our many nonprofit outreach programs, please visit www.guidepostsfoundation.org.